The Book of
North Newton

THE BOOK OF
NORTH NEWTON

IN CELEBRATION OF A SOMERSET PARISH

J.C. ROBINS AND K.C. ROBINS

HALSGROVE

First published in Great Britain in 1999

British Library Cataloguing-in-Publication Data
A CIP record for this title is available from the British Library

ISBN 1 84114 042 2

HALSGROVE
PUBLISHING, MEDIA AND DISTRIBUTION

Halsgrove House
Lower Moor Way
Tiverton, Devon EX16 6SS
Tel: 01884 243242
Fax: 01884 243325
website: http://www.halsgrove.com

Printed and bound in Great Britain by Bookcraft Ltd, Midsomer Norton

CONTENTS

Durston Station, c.1900. Though beyond the parish boundary, the station has had a great impact on the lives of the parishioners.

ACKNOWLEDGEMENTS

This book would not have been possible without the help, enthusiasm and support given by the inhabitants of North Newton Parish, those of today and yesterday. Special thanks are expressed to those who have lent photographs and memorabilia, and remembered how things were years ago:

Jim Addicott, Ray and Una Barham, Ruby Barrington, Graham and Pauline Bartlett, Penny Berry, John and Margaret Boyer, Alan Bradford, Gerald Bramley, Jean Brookes, Geoffrey Broughton, James Broughton, Vivien Broughton, Heather Brown, Colin and Lorraine Burr, Frank Clegg, Cuthbert Coate, Pat Collard, Mary Collard-Jenkins, Sue Collard-Jenkins, Diane Coram, Wendy Darch, Linda Defriez, Colin Duddridge, Frank Duddridge, Jean Duddridge, John Durman, Sybil Edwards, Mr Farthing, Gordon Finnimore, Joyce Foster, Anne and Gordon Fraser, Lady Gass, David Gliddon, Mark Goodwin, Anne Guerin, Carol Habberfield, the Habberfield family of Banklands, Robin Harris, R. Hill, Sylvia Hillman, Ann and Geoff Holt, Helen Jeffries, Len and Daisy Kitts, Christopher and Mary Lorimer, Kathy Lowe, Linda Lowndes, John Marchant, Janet and Chris Patten, Les Pickersgill, John Pike, Reg Price, Revd Rosemary Radcliffe, Graham Reading, Pat Richards, Gerald Rossiter, Trevor Sellick, Sir Benjamin Slade, Andrew Smith, Ian and Penny Smith, Edward Stone, Dr Richard Williams, Peter Windo, Marian Woods, North Newton Women's Institute. Special thanks to Sue Pottle for proof reading the text and to Sandy Florés for supplying the delightful sketches of North Newton.

In addition, the following were consulted:

Victorian History of Somerset, *Burke's Peerage*, *History of Somerset* by Collinson, *The Forests of Somerset* by Gresswell, *History of Somerset* by Robert Dunning, *Somerset at War* by Mac Hawkins, *By Waterway to Taunton* by Tony Haskell, *Somerset Parks and Gardens* by James Bond, *Buildings of England – South & West Somerset* by N. Pevsner, *Notes on the Parish of North Petherton* by A.B. Marchant, *A Short Account of the Church and Parish of St Peter* by Rev. L.H. King, *Dictionary of National Biography*, *Somerset Paupers – Unremembered Lives* by Thelma Munkton, *The Life of Geoffrey Chaucer* by D. Pearsall, *Somerset* by Robin Bush, local newspapers, including the *Bridgwater Mercury* and the *Bristol Post*, Somerset Archaeology and Natural History Society, Somerset Record Office and Somerset Local Studies Library.

One of the original swing bridges on the Bridgwater to Taunton Canal.

North Newton Village School and the Old Vicarage viewed from the open ground now occupied by the Harvest Moon public house, c.1900.

FOREWORD

Of the early history of North Newton, we may not know a great deal beyond the fact that its roots have been traced back to Celtic times and beyond. What we do know however, is that the parish of North Newton originated, in common with the majority of rural hamlets, as a small community where daily life revolved around the working of the land and the bringing up and supporting of families.

Such communities were close knit. Through mutual co-operation and close connections with one another, a real sense of identity ensured that the members of the parish found strength from one another when, at times, life was perhaps not so easy. To some extent, this sense of identity and friendship is in danger of being diluted with increasing urbanisation and the development of the countryside. However, the individual nature of the parish of North Newton survives and through producing this book, the authors are attempting to regenerate the strong community spirit of the past and to build up a clearer picture of North Newton leading up to the year 2000.

Instead of looking at history through the eyes of an outsider, the standpoint of the book is that of those born within, and heavily associated with, the area. Much support has been given by those who have come forward with photographs, documents and first-hand memories of 'the old days' and I hope that all who read the book will both enjoy it and learn some new nugget of information about North Newton.

It is perhaps apt to remind ourselves that during the hustle and bustle of life as we enter the new millennium, we should not take the countryside and its attributes for granted – a truism reflected upon by William Henry Davies in 'Leisure':

> What is this life, if full of care,
> We have no time to stand and stare.
> No time to stand beneath the boughs
> And stare as long as sheep or cows.
> A poor life this if, full of care,
> We have no time to stand and stare.

Sir Benjamin Slade, 7th Baronet of Maunsel House
North Newton, Somerset

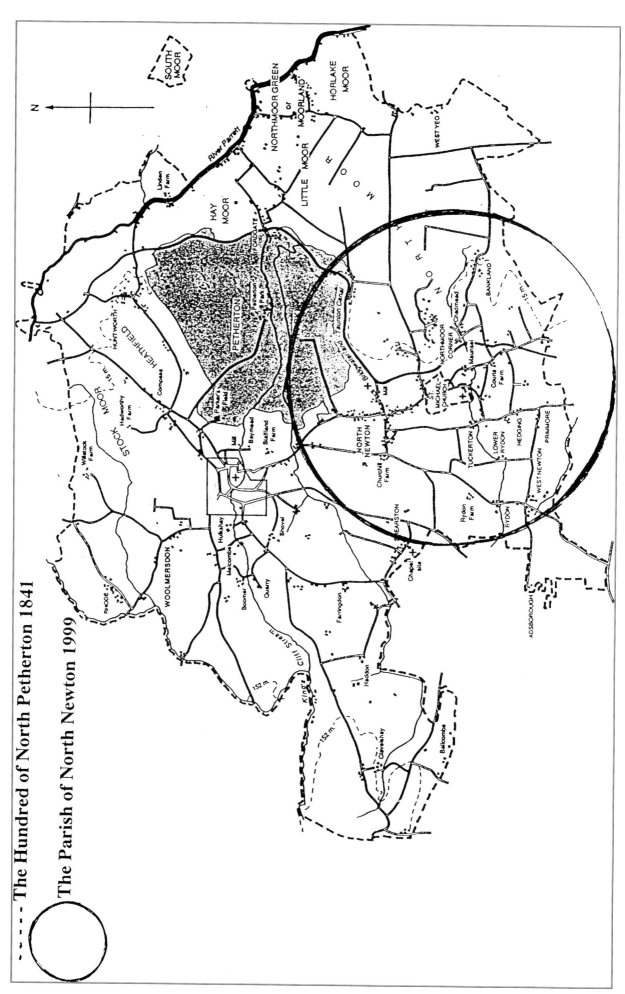

The Hundred of North Petherton 1841

The Parish of North Newton 1999

10

INTRODUCTION

The parish of North Newton lies south of North Petherton, in the heart of Somerset between the county town of Taunton and the industrial town of Bridgwater. The course of the Bridgwater to Taunton canal runs along the west side of the village with the Somerset Levels stretching out to the east.

As we approach the millennium, we notice more than ever how the parish has changed and developed over the years – under the influence of the surrounding landscape, the trials and tribulations of the wealthier landowners and, in particular, with the technological advancements of the last 100 years. The intervention of modern machinery has forced the traditional working methods to be cast aside. The lives of the parishioners have also undergone dramatic change, some having moved away to seek their fortunes, to be replaced by 'newcomers' wishing to make North Newton their home, thus keeping the sense of community alive.

At the beginning of 1998, John and I (*below*) felt that we should do something to celebrate the millennium which could be of interest to ourselves and the people linked with the parish. That 'something' became this book!

Little did we know, at the time, what we were letting ourselves in for. John has always had an interest in history and since coming to live in North Newton 16 years ago has enjoyed building up his knowledge of the locality. The challenge of writing a book presented itself at the right time. I am working full time so knew that my help would be sporadic. Once he reached the point of gathering information from individuals and getting them involved by supplying photographs and memories, etc. this was where I came in. In some respects the information has been overwhelming and we have not been able to include everything. Life never stands still for long (even in the heart of Somerset!) and we acknowledge that changes may occur in the village between completion of the manuscript and publication. We have, however, made every endeavour to ensure that facts are correct at the time of going to press.

We needed to undertake a great deal of research into the history of the area and this became John's first priority. Reginald Price who has lived in the village all his life was of particular help. As a hobby, Reg had collated information over a number of years, all of which was carefully documented and filed. He has given us access to this information which is now in our safe-keeping with a promise that, one day, it will be passed on to the Somerset Record Office. Hopefully, 18 months on, the end product will be an enjoyable read for everyone.

Kay Robins
Penrod, North Newton
July 1999

IN SOMERSETSHIRE.

Particulars and Conditions of Sale

OF ONE OF THE MOST COMPACT

Freehold Estates

WITHIN THE

COUNTY OF SOMERSET.

IT INCLUDES

1,250 ACRES OF LAND,

Entirely within a Ring Fence,

DIVIDED INTO

FOUR EXCEEDINGLY FINE FARMS,

In the occupation of most respectable Tenants, at Rents approaching to

£3,000 PER ANNUM,

And this at a considerably reduced Rental. The situation is quite equal to the most favoured part of Somersetshire; it is close to

NORTH PETHERTON,

In the Rich Vale between Bridgewater and Taunton, and

CLOSE TO THE TURNPIKE ROAD.

The Farm-Houses present a refreshing contrast to many throughout the County; and the whole (excepting a Field or two) is

FREE FROM TITHES;

It will be Sold by Auction

BY

Mr. GEO^E. ROBINS

At the AUCTION MART, LONDON,

On THURSDAY, AUGUST 8, 1833, at Twelve o'Clock,

IN ONE LOT.

Particulars may be had at the George Inn, North Petherton; Hotel, Bridgewater; the Castle, Taunton; the New and Old London Inns, Exeter; the York House, Bath; of Mr. RANDOLPH, Solicitor, Milverton, Somerset; Messrs. JONES and CAREW, Solicitors, Exeter; R. B. FOLLETT, Solicitor, Temple; Messrs. KARSLAKE and CREALOCK, Solicitors, Regent Street; the Auction Mart; and at Mr. GEORGE ROBINS's Offices, Covent Garden, London.

THOMAS RICH will attend to show the Estate.   Whiting, Beaufort House, Strand.

Above: *Manor House Farm and Park House Farm (formerly Petherton Park).*

Left: *Details of sale of Petherton Park in 1833.*

Chapter 1: Early History

North Newton boasts a rich history. Until the late 19th century it was part of the hundred of North Petherton. It evolved from a Saxon settlement and has links with Alfred the Great through a succession of family estates – many of which held the Forestership-in-Fee of Petherton Park. Some had royal and parliamentarian connections (such as the Mortimer and Wroth families) and, with the sale of most of the estates from the 18th century, made it the community it is today.

Good soil and a plentiful supply of wood and water attracted man to the area thousands of years ago: it appears that the area of North Newton was settled in the Stone Age. In 1973, during the construction of the M5 motorway, evidence of a Mesolithic (middle phase of the Stone Age) settlement was found near Greenway Farm, Moon Lane, and evidence of Romano-British settlement has also been found at three sites – one in North Newton opposite Puffers Cottage on the Petherton road, one at West Newton near West Newton Farm, and one at Hedging Barton.

In the 5th century, the Angles (a tribe of German origin, who became known as the English) settled in England. It is suggested that the Angles may have had a primitive landing-site at, or near, English Gate which gave them access to the moorland (at this time an inland sea).

There are indications that the Celts were also early settlers, in particular in the naming of Michaelchurch. St Michael was the patron saint of the Celts and the church at Michaelchurch bears his name (as do a number of others in the locality, including St Michaels Tower on Glastonbury Tor). Celtic wheat has been recovered, grown and harvested in trials using the old methods, and apparently produced about the same yield as the farming methods of today.

The first true settlers were the Saxons, who were not only hunters but who worked the land with their tools. The suffix 'ton' is a derivative of the Saxon place name 'tun', the broadest definition of which is 'an enclosure or a small patch of land with dwellings enclosed within a hedge or a wall'. The Domesday Book of 1086 shows how strongly the Saxons had settled in this area and mentions five holdings bearing the name Newton.

The evolution of the village was closely associated with that of the royal forests of the county. Petherton (or Newton) Park was the largest and most important of the King's five royal forests in Somerset, and North Newton appears to lie on a route between Clavelshay and the Quantocks and Petherton Park, so from the 12th century was probably the latter's administration centre.

The *Victorian History of Somerset* states: 'By 1066 Newton had been divided into five manors which, by 1086, totalled 9.5 ploughlands'. Records show that in Edward the Confessor's time (1042-66), the most important official in Newton was the Provost, Osward, who resided at Newton Regis (or Newton Court). Osward was succeeded by Ansketil the Parker, the forester for Petherton, who is shown in the Domesday Book as holding Newton for the king. This shows that the North Newton link with the forest of Petherton goes back well over 900 years and that it was probably one of only two Somerset parks mentioned in the Domesday Book. Legend has it that Alfred 'burnt the cakes' near his stately court at Newton Court (or Newton Regis as it was sometimes called), a connection which has been reinforced with the discovery of the Alfred Jewel – perhaps one of the most celebrated artifacts to have survived from Anglo-Saxon England. It was found in 1693 in Parkers Field, near the manor of Petherton (Newton) Park. In 1730, Thomas Palmer, the son of the jewel's original owner, referred to Petherton Park as 'the park and manor of Newenton'. Robin Bush reinforces this in *Somerset – A Portrait in Colour*, by stating that it was found at Sir Thomas Wrothe's Petherton Park in North Newton.

These settlements grew gradually over the passing decades and in the late 12th century they were combined by William Wrotham. He named the estate 'Newton Forester' and included Petherton Park. This was the precursor to the village of North Newton. In 1298 Newton Forester is shown as a village with deforestation under way. The Plessis family renamed it in the late 13th century and over several centuries the name of Newton has appeared in historical documents as Newentone, with the added confusion of Plessey being changed to Plessis, Plecy, Placy and Plessetis. Only by the late 18th century had it become known (for the most part) as North Newton.

In 1283 the village was split into three manors – Newton Regis (which contained Petherton Park), Newton Wroth and Newton Chantry. In 1553, Newton Wroth and Newton Regis were united by Sir Thomas Wroth, remaining under the control of his family until 1722. With the death of Sir Thomas Wroth, the title became extinct and the estates passed into the hands of the Acland family, through the marriage of Sir Thomas' niece to Sir

Hugh Acland. Newton Regis and Newton Wroth became the old manors in the village. The Day and Masters Map of 1782 shows the village as North Newton.

There is much controversy as to whether Petherton Park was part of North Petherton or North Newton and to add to the confusion over the correct name, various historians have used both. The *Victorian History of Somerset* further complicates matters by suggesting that Newton was a separate park by 1339. The area south of the church had been divided and let by 1671. Evidence appears to point to the fact that Petherton Park was part of one of the manors of North Newton (probably known as Newton Regis) with its administration centre at a manor house on the edge of Parkers Field. By the early 16th century, this manor house had been superseded by a new manor, initially called Broad Lodge which, in the 17th century, was rebuilt by the Wroth family to become the manor house of North Newton, Petherton Park. Today the property is known as Manor House Farm and Park House Farm.

These royal forests contributed to the Royal Exchequer from the revenues of the forest courts, the selling of forest rights and foresterships-in-fee. The park may have been walled in the early 14th century to hold deer, and was approximately four miles in circumference. Entrances were at Fordgate, Huntworth Gate, English Gate and probably at North Newton and Heathfield Gate. By the 17th century the forest and parkland had disappeared.

In 1193, it had been under the wardenship (given by William the Conqueror) of Count Robert Auberville and his descendents, also shown as Osberville or de Odburville, who originated from Caen, France. In 1198, Richard I (the Lionheart) granted all the Aubervill estates to William de Wrotham (son of Geoffrey de Wrotham who had been a servant to several Archbishops of Canterbury):

Richard, by the grace of God, King of England to his Archbishops, Bishops, Abbots, Earls, Barons, Justices, Sheriffs, Stewards, Reeves, officers, All his bailiffs and trusty men, Greetings.

Know ye that we have granted, given and by our present charter have confirmed to William de Wrotham for the homage and service, all the lands and tenements which Robert de Osberville held in Newton.

Wherefore we will and strictly order that the aforesaid William and his heirs after him may have and hold all the aforesaid tenements by the said service of one Knight's fee for every service in woods and fields, waters, ponds, mills, stews, fisheries.

Given by the hand of Eustace, Bishop of Ely, and Chancellor, at Leon, the twenty five day of August, ninth year of our reign (25 August 1198).

Wrotham family control was to last around 150 years. In the late 13th century the village was renamed Newentone Plessey (or Placy) by the then owner, Richard de Plessis (a great nephew of William Wrotham). Richard died in 1289 without issue and the estate was split into three parts. His three sisters each inherited a third of the estate, one of whom, Sabina Peche, became the only lady warden of the Somerset Forests. Mathew Peche was the last descendent of William de Wrotham to hold the hereditary Forestership. In about 1341 the Wrotham links were severed when Mathew Peche sold the office, together with the Newton property, to Sir Richard Damory (or Dammory) thus ending the 150 years of the Wrotham family inheritance of the Forestership of Somerset.

From 1341 to 1460, the office of the Forestership of the Somerset Forests passed through many hands. In 1351, it was sold to Sir Roger de Beauchamp for the sum of 100 marks of silver. In 1359, he sold it to Roger Mortimer, Earl of March, for double that amount – not a bad investment even by today's standards! The Earl was unable to make the best of his purchase, however, as he died in France in 1360. The office was held directly by the Mortimer family until the death of Edmund the 5th Earl of March in 1425 and whilst under the Mortimers' control, the foresters were generally substitutionary officers, acting with considerable authority. Two of these substitutes in the late 14th century and early 15th century were Geoffrey Chaucer ('Father of English poetry' and author of The Canterbury Tales) and Thomas Chaucer, his son. Historians are divided over Geoffrey Chaucer's involvement in the Park. Some say that he lived in Park House in Park House Field, now known as Parkers Field. This was probably the lodge which housed the foresters and which the historian, Leland, noted in the early 16th century was surrounded by a moat. Others say that that it is unlikely that he ever lived in or even visited Somerset. There is no doubt that he was appointed Deputy Forester in the 1390s and it may have been for two periods, in the early and late '90s. These years were said to be a period of pecuniary discomfort for Chaucer. He had been dismissed in 1391 from his position as Clerk of the King's Works and before being appointed by Roger Mortimer to the sinecure post of Sub-Forester, he had to survive on a pension of £10 per annum. Derek Pearsall, in his 1992 book on Chaucer, says that the post 'was quasi-legal and very boring, and we are not to imagine him traversing the woodland rides of Somerset, or living or probably even visiting there'. Others, like the 18th-century historian, the Revd Gresswell, suggested that some of the characters of the *Prologue* were based on people that Chaucer had met during his period as Forester at Petherton Park. For example, the Prioress was probably based on his neighbour, the head of the Nunnery at nearby Mynchin Buckland. The *Prologue* also gives a contemporary picture of a yeoman forester. The truth is a matter for speculation, but documents of the time show that Chaucer lived throughout the 1390s in Kent. This does not rule out the possibility that he came to Somerset, but points to the fact that any visit would probably have been short.

On the death of Edmund Mortimer in 1425, the Forestership and the Manor of Newton Plessey passed to his nephew, Richard of Cambridge, the Duke of York (who was still a minor). On his death in 1460, his own son and heir became Edward the IV on 4 March 1461, and the office of the Forestership of the Somerset Forests became extinct, the estates passing to the Crown and to Edward's daughters. Thus ended an office that had roots in Saxon times and its origin in Saxon 'forest custom'. It had been an important office not only because of the illustrious personages who filled it and its association with the Mortimer family, but also because of the historical links it furnished. The picture of Alfred at Newton Court shows the historical significance of Petherton Park. Gresswell suggested that there was never a single forest in England that played a greater part in guiding the history and wars of England than Petherton Park in 878. He also said that it was a pity there is no memorial of a lasting kind at North Newton to remind us of the events that took place there.

In 1547, the lordship was granted to Edward Seymour, Duke of Somerset. Following his attainment he was condemned to death for treason and had to forfeit his estates. The lordship was then granted to John Dudley, Duke of Northumberland, who, in the same year exchanged it for Syon House in Middlesex owned by Sir Thomas Wroth. So started an association with the Wroth family which was to last for over 170 years.

The Wroths were descendants of an ancient family who lived at Blenden Hall, at Boxley in Kent, and some of whom later took up residence in Newton Plessey. Revd Collinson wrote that, although some members of the family lived at Durants at Enfield in Middlesex, descendants in the time of Queen Elizabeth I pulled down the Park House and used the material to build a manor house called Broad Lodge. This was rebuilt,

Sir Thomas Wroth, 3rd Baronet (c.1675-1721) of Petherton Park, from a portrait by J. Hawkerm 1696. Reproduced by kind permission of the Somerset Archaeological and Natural History Society.

became Petherton Park, and the parklands were converted to farms. In the early 1950s, this property was subsequently divided and became Manor Farm and Park House Farm.

It was probably also during this period that deforestation was accelerated. Wood was extremely profitable, having a great many uses other than for fuel. It had always been in demand as a building material for houses, wagons, ships, etc. and in the 13th century wood from Newton Park was the source of much of the timber granted by the king. In 1230, six furcas (forked trees used in the construction of roofs) went to Godfrey de Crocombe for building a barn and in 1278, three oaks went to Somerton to repair a belfry. Wood was also used for building work at Bridgwater and Stogursey Castles, Somerton Gaol, Cleeve and Glastonbury Abbeys, Buckland Priory, the roof of North Petherton Church, the houses of friars in Bridgwater, Ilchester and Somerton, and Bridgwater churches. Timber was supplied from Newton Park for fine woodwork – in 1232, two oaks for choirstalls at Cleeve Abbey and in 1250, three oaks for making images for the Abbey Church of Glastonbury.

Dead trees, fallen wood and undergrowth also provided fuel. The sisters of Minchin Buckland received a series of grants of dead wood, thorn, buck-thorn and maple from Newton Park in 1229, an event which was often repeated in later years. Sales of timber provided a steady income to the estate, upwards of £200 per annum in the 1580s, but approximately 140 of the best oaks were destroyed during the Civil War. As urbanisation began to increase and with a rapid growth in the population, demand rose dramatically, especially in the late 1700s. This also put greater pressure on agriculture to produce more timber and the old paternalistic system died out in most areas as a capitalistic, entrepreneurial, market-led economy took its place. Farming became big business and the old way of life all but disappeared. By 1610, a map by Speed showed that much of the Royal Forest of North Petherton had been 'enclosed'.

The Wroth family ownership continued for 172 years, until the death (without male issue), of Sir Thomas Wroth in 1722 at the age of 47. During this time, the Wroth influence, power and land expanded, for in addition to land in North Newton, they also owned land in North

Petherton, Monkton and Creech St Michael. By 1672, the Wroths had control of two-thirds of the original estate. The Manor of Newton Wroth descended with Newton Regis (although Newton Plecy had effectively combined at an earlier date when a previous Sir Thomas Wroth left Newton Wroth to his wife in the late 16th century). Sir Thomas Wroth also bought the whole of the estate at Bankland and Chadmead in the early 18th century. He was Member of Parliament for Bridgwater and Wells and was also the Sheriff of Somerset from 1708-09. His children married into the local aristocracy, e.g. the Acland and Tonge families. They rebuilt the Free Chapel of Newentone Placy (St Peters Church in North Newton) on the site of the Chantry built by Richard Plessis for 'the health of his soul and for the souls of his father and mother' and they also set up the Wroth Charity. According to Collinson, Sir Thomas died at Kellerton (Killerton), Devon, in 1721. He and several members of the Wroth family are buried at St Peters (although no records appear for them in the graveyard). A substantial memorial to Sir Thomas can be seen in Stogursey Church, which confirms that he was buried at North Newton.

The parish records show that he was buried on 25 July 1721, but there is no lasting memorial in St Peters, which is rather strange. (An earlier member of the family, William, was buried in Bridgwater Parish Church.). The Wroth family had their own pew, known as Park Pew, in North Petherton Church and this had an entry from the south porch in order that their servants could provide them with refreshments during the long sermons of the 18th century. On the death of Sir Thomas, the title became extinct and the estates were divided up between Sir Hugh Acland (who was married to Sir Thomas' eldest daughter, Cecily) and his nephew, Nathaniel Palmer. In her book *A Devon Family*, Anne Acland writes that it was a magnificent match which 'much hastened

Above: *Memorial to Sir Thomas Wroth in Stogursey Parish Church (by kind permission of the vicar of Stogursey Church).*

Opposite page: *A porch notice in St Michaelchurch on parish poor relief.*

the Aclands' return to prosperity'. Cecily's dowry brought in a cash endowment of £12 000 and, with the death of her father, 2300 acres of land. The estates of Newton Wroth and Newton Regis thus passed into the control of the Acland family.

Sir Hugh Acland died a young man in 1728 and his five-year-old son, Thomas, inherited the property and title. In 1744, he made his home at Petherton Park and in 1745 followed his father's example by marrying a woman who was richer

This Table is sacred to the Memory, Of S.ᵗ THOMAS WROTH *Bar.*;
Late of *PETHERTON PARK* in the County of *SOMERSET*;
Who by his own inherent Virtue, Added Dignity to the Honour derived From a very ancient Lineage;
Who served his Country many Years in Parliament, With uncorrupted Fidelity;
As Representative for the Town of *BRIDGEWATER*, the City of *WELLS*, & County of *SOMERSET*
And in the Seafons of Retirement from Publick Busine∫s, Cheer'd and enliven'd his Neighbourhood,
With the Generous Spirit of Ancient English Hospitality.
He was a Tender Father, a con∫tant, obliging Husband, A perfectly Humane, & Honeft Man.
At length having pa∫sed well through the Honours & Employments of this Life,
He was advanced to the Rewards of a better,
He dyed the 25.ᵗʰ of June 1721 Aged 46
His Remains were deposited at *NEWTON* in the Parish of *PETHERTON*,
His Memory still survives.

Inscription on the memorial to Sir Thomas Wroth (by kind permission of the vicar of Stogursey Church).

than himself, she being Elizabeth Dyke of Tetton, near Taunton. This marriage brought him three new estates in Somerset and a substantial amount of money. Lady Acland died in 1753, leaving two sons, John and Thomas. In 1770, Petherton Park was settled on the eldest, John, when he married. John died in 1778 at the age of 34 (having just returned from the American War of Independence), leaving a string of debts behind him. The estate then passed to his son, another John, who died in 1785 at the age of nine. The estate then passed to his uncle, Sir Thomas Dyke Acland, who was also well known for getting into debt. This was such a problem that by 1784 his father felt compelled to make a will, allowing Sir Thomas no access to capital, and everything was left 'in trust' to his descendants. Thomas did not live at Petherton Park but when he died in 1794 the Trustees had to sell a great part of the estate to pay his debts. Parish records show that a number of the Acland family were interred in the Chancery of St Peters from 1761 to 1806 but, as with the Wroth family, no reference appears in the church.

The village of North Newton we see today (then known as Newentone Plessey or Placey) began to take its shape from this time. It was enclosed with smallholdings and farms, many of which still exist. In 1833, Sir Thomas Acland sold most of the Petherton Park estate to William Cordington Nation, a barrister and magistrate, of Rockbeare House, Exeter, together with its five farms – Impens, Park, Standards, Fordgate and Parkers Field, a total of 1253 acres for the grand sum of £79 200.

William Nation died in 1861, and his son, another William, inherited the estate. The 1841 Tithe Map showed that the Aclands only owned about 480 acres, mostly around the village of North Newton. There were three other major landowners also shown on the map: Sir John Slade, William Nation and the Vicars Choral of Wells, i.e. the Church.

Up until 1888, North Newton and the surrounding area came within the hundred of North Petherton, which had overall administration and judicial responsibility. However, up until the 17th century the organ for local government was largely in the hands of the lords of the manor. By the middle of the 17th century most manorial courts had been superseded by Justices of the Peace, one of whom was Sir Thomas Wroth.

It is highly likely that the village had stocks, a pillory, a whipping post and a ducking stool to mete out punishment to offenders and it is thought that the stocks were near the site of the school as it was once known as Stocks Corner. The village also had a pound, as did West Newton. Up until the early 19th century the parish was responsible for supporting the old, the sick and the insane, and for providing work for the unemployed in workhouses. A workhouse was built in North Petherton in 1737-38, probably in the High Street near Tappers Lane, and this eventually became an annexe to the main workhouse in Bridgwater. Records from 1836 show 185 paupers in the parish and their charge to the rates:

Indoor paupers	*£5.18s.2d.*
Outdoor paupers	*£325.16s.7d.*
Establishment Charges	*£6.18s.2d.*
Total Charges	*£449.18s.2d.*

Those poor who did not qualify for poor relief had to rely on 'gifts' such as the gift bequeathed by William Brown, in 1766, of an annual sum of £2 to be used to buy and distribute bread to the poor of North Newton who were not receiving relief from the parish on St Stephens Day (26 December). Some 40 shillings per year was also bequeathed in John Slade's will to provide tools for the poor (*below*). Others, such as the Revd Toogood in North Petherton, organised distribution of bread to the poor from the Wrothe Charity in 1836. Also, in the same year, he gave his own Christmas gift to the poor, buying 40 lbs of beef for £2, making it into 63 gallons of soup with carrots, onions and other vegetables and distributing it to more than 250 people – nearly 10 per cent of the parish.

The average wage of the farm labourer at this time would have been between 9 and 10 shillings per week plus a daily allowance of cider. Carters and shepherds received a shilling a week more, but were expected to work more than the ten-hour day of the labourers. Women were paid 7 to 8 pence per day for work in the fields. The *Taunton Courier* in March 1833 reported that:

Lady Slade, always alive to the needs of the poor, gave, at Easter, 200 pieces of beef, with bread in proportion, to those immediately around Maunsel; and on Easter Monday, according to custom, twenty of the labourers were regaled with roast beef and plum pudding, with plenty of strong beer and punch in the servants' hall.

17

In 1880 it is estimated that there were at least 80 paupers in and around the village and a Friendly Society was formed to relieve their suffering. This society had been part of the North Petherton Friendly Society, but an independent group was formed when North Newton became a separate parish in 1880. Its aims were to 'raise and sustain a fund to assist sick and infirm members and provide decent burials for its members'. The Society/Club held an annual Festival Day on the third Tuesday in May. It is said that villagers went pea-picking in the morning and to the club celebrations in the afternoon. It is not known when the society was disbanded, but a surviving photograph shows that it was still in existence in 1908.

It is difficult to give an accurate figure for the population before the first census of 1801 and even this is likely to be something of a guess. However, estimates can be made which show that the population has increased over the years. In 1086 the recorded number in the parish/hundred was 172 with 66 of these at the Royal Manor of North Petherton, thus leaving the remaining 106 spread among the other 12 estates. Population density was of the order of 10-20 people per square mile. If we look at the five estates mentioned in the Domesday Book which were to form North Newton, an estimated figure for the population of the village would probably be in the region of 50-60 when these estates amalgamated. In 1563 only 13 houses were recorded in North Newton out of a total of 236 in the parish. Again it is difficult to estimate the village population using this information, but a figure of around 50-60 would

be a reasonable estimate. In 1667 nearly 320 people were recorded in the North Newton tithing, which extended outside the parish. If the village followed the national trend, then it is likely that the population would have almost doubled to around 120. By 1801 the population of the parish was 2346 and the 1841 census shows that the population of the 'hamlet of North Newton' was 280 occupying 55 houses.

Some families lived in overcrowded conditions. George Clatworthy, tailor, and George Browning, shoemaker, each lived in a cottage with their respective wives and troops of seven children. The 1881 census showed that there were now 75 properties in the village and an increased population of approximately 340. By 1891 there were 85 properties in the village, but the population had dropped to around 328.

Despite this apparent increase in housing, overcrowding remained a problem; William Bond, a market gardener, lived with his wife and ten children in a house in Church Road (where the census showed there to be six consecutive houses occupied by widows).

In 1881, the population (including that of the surrounding hamlets of West Newton, Tuckerton, Banklands, Hedging, etc.) was 750. It peaked in 1891 to 785 but dropped steadily to 464 in 1990. It now appears to be rising again, with a figure of 569 having been reached in 1998, reflecting the increase in building which has occurred in the parish, especially in North Newton. It is estimated that at least 47 new houses have been built in or around the village since about 1980.

North Newton Friendly Society Festival 1908.

Chapter 2: Trade and Industry

MILLS

There appear to have been at least five mills in and around the village. Lower Mill, close to the Maunsel Estate, was recorded in 1631, and was described in 1770 as 'lying by the canals in the grounds of Maunsel House'. It was disused by 1838, when it became a lodge called 'The Dairy'. Today it is known as Dairy Mead Cottage.

Another mill in St Michaelchurch, dating from the 13th century, is Maunsel Mill, which appears to have stopped operating by the 1930s. Traces of walling to divert water to a higher level suggest that the watercourse was not a natural one. The mill has now been converted into a house but the remains of the overshot wheel and the machinery survive and are a feature of the conversion.

North Newton Mill was attached to Newton Plecy Manor. It was recorded in 1274, rebuilt in 1356-7 and repairs were made to the mill equipment in 1360. It was let during the 15th century, but by the 1480s had fallen into disrepair. By the late 16th century it appeared to be part of Newton Regis Manor although the Wroths continued to 'owe suit' for the mill to the Vicars Choral for their share and reserved the right to have their grain ground free for two weeks every year. In 1758 the Aclands leased the mill and all its surrounding property for £22 to George King (who we know was still the miller in 1809 as he appears on the Tithe Map). A new mill brook was made in 1799 but the mill was later converted to steam power, then changed to diesel power before going out of use in c.1945. The owner at that time was Harvey Johnson, an RAF officer who kept an aeroplane at

Impens. He set up in business as a corn merchant and also opened up a battery farm in the adjacent field – now owned by Lloyd Maunder Ltd. The mill was dismantled in the early 1960s, but the Mill House remains and is now occupied by the Fraser family. The 1891 census shows that the miller was Charles Heal, members of whose family also occupied Great House at the time, one George Heal being shown in the census as a farmer. By 1906 however, the census shows George Heal as the miller while confusingly *Kelly's Directory* of the same year lists him as a cattle dealer and farmer (while the miller, meanwhile, is shown as John Alfred Woolley). In 1910, Edmund Habberfield became the miller, also starting up a bakery business. The mill was bought by the Baker brothers in 1924 and was managed, until his death in 1935, by Philip Baker. William Trunks was then employed by Walter Baker to run the mill which was closed down in 1941 when he sold the business.

A fourth mill operated in Petherton Park in the 1670s but had disappeared by 1838 (although the field name 'Mill Close' survives south of Park Farm). There was also a mill at Rydon, but again nothing of this establishment survives.

Above: *Maunsel Mill*
Left: *Dairy Mead Cottage*

North Newton Mill c.1900.

A Christmas card sent from Harvey Johnson (former owner of North Newton Mill) to the Harvest Moon.

BRIDGWATER TO TAUNTON CANAL

The canal was opened in 1827 and provided employment for boatmen and lock-keepers alike. Among them were James Bartlett and Thomas Bennett in 1891 and, of course, Frank Duddridge at Standards Lock after the Second World War. The waterway was used extensively by farmers to transport produce, and was so valued that the sale documents for Petherton Park in 1833 made a point of the virtue of the canal for this purpose. Landowners also benefited from the sale of their land due to the construction of the canal. Sir John Acland was offered £95 per acre for two acres and one rood, together with timber from the edges of the land for the price of £223.15s. Richard King of Sellicks Farm, 'part and parcel of Newton Place', was paid £174 for the purchase of 'three roods and ten perches of land at Slow Meadow, taken for the purposes of the said canal, together with the land tax and also the tithes of corn, grain and hay'.

Although reasonably successful in the early years, the company was unable to compete with the railways, which, in 1842, had opened a link between Bridgwater and Taunton. Burdened by high interest repayments and decreasing trade the Canal Company (which also owned Bridgwater Docks) went into receivership in the early 1850s and, ironically, was bought by the Bristol and Exeter Railway

Above: *The view approaching Standards Lock.*
Below: *Cleaning weed from the canal.*

Company for £64 000 in 1866. Trade on the canal continued, but due to lack of maintenance and, at times, of water, the canal was closed to commercial traffic in 1907. It remained navigable by small craft until 1939.

In 1989, after over 40 years of neglect, the canal was once more made accessible to leisure traffic, when the first section of the restored waterway was opened between Bridgwater and North Newton. Since then, it has been fully opened to Taunton (and the canal towpath is also part of a national cycle route). Today Maunsel Lock Cottage is the only remaining lock cottage on the canal. Lovingly restored by Sylvia and Tony Rymell, it is now run by the couple as a small waterside business, known as the Maunsel Canal Centre, for the benefit of the canal and its visitors.

Village children used to swim in the canal and John Pike, who now lives in Brislington, near Bristol, is the grandson of Eli Pike, who used to run a market garden at Randells Farm. John remembers learning to swim in the canal and paying a shilling per year to use a hut for changing at Kings Lock. He also remembers the time that the canal dried up and the annual check of the waterway by the Canal Company officials who threw coins to the children on the bank. Ex lock-keeper, Frank Duddridge, also recalls this annual event, and being showered with pennies from the men in top hats.

Top: *Installing the new swing bridge at North Newton, 1990.*

Above: *The canal was also used for annual raft races. Here raft racing takes place in 1977 to celebrate the Silver Jubilee.*

Above: *The remaining lock-keepers cottage at Maunsel Lock.*

Left: *An outing on the canal.*

CLOTH

Cloth was manufactured in the parish in the 1400s and many craftsmen were employed in this industry during the 17th and 18th centuries, the main product being serge. Records of 1667 show that there were four weavers in North Newton – some, no doubt, augmenting the income from their craft with farming, brewing or cider making.

RETAILERS

The late 20th century has witnessed the widespread demise of 'the village shop' and North Newton has been no exception.

Records show that in the 17th century there was a shoemaker in the village who had not one but two shops. This was probably John Bobbett who died in 1688, his estate being valued at £39. In one shop he sold his own products and in the other, a 'ware' shop, he stocked fruit, sugar, tobacco and brandy. By the 19th century, most of the villages surrounding North Petherton had their own shops, smithies and craftsmen. There were three butchers, three bakers (no candlestick makers!), a grocer and a shopkeeper in North Newton. A 'master' machine maker was recorded in the village and there was a foundry at Hedging. *Kelly's Directory* of 1897 lists Robert Hubbard (established for 25 years) as a coach and carriage builder, general wheelwright, carpenter and smith, wagon, van, cart and lorry builder (so he must have been a busy man). In 1906 he was still in business in Petherton Road but the concern was later taken over by Frank Culliford. In 1918 George Reading's bill-heads advertised his business thus: 'wheelwright, waggon, cart and lorry builders, carpenters and undertakers'.

An examination of *Kelly's Directories* from 1883 to 1935 shows how the village and surrounding hamlets, whilst remaining quite overwhelmingly dependent on agriculture, became less and less self-sufficient as the commercial infrastructure declined. In 1883, the situation appears to have been a healthy one. There were at least ten commercial enterprises in the village – bakers, blacksmiths, a shopkeeper, a miller, a wheelwright, a butcher, a carpenter, bootmaker, tailor and haulier (and there were also 22 farmers and 10 market gardeners). By 1889, a Post Office appeared in the village, running a limited service in the home of the boot-maker, William Whitehead, at Smithy Cottage, and William is shown as Sub Postmaster in 1894 with increased duties (he could now issue postal orders, but not cash them). By 1897, the number of commercial enterprises had increased and business still appears to have been doing well. In addition to the above, Mark and Charles Dunn traded as builders and masons and there were agricultural machinery businesses, Walter Adams and James House being cattle/sheep dealers. The number of businessmen within certain trades also increased, there being two bakers, two blacksmiths and two carpenters.

However, from the beginning of the 20th century numbers started slowly to decline. By 1910 there were no tailors or boot-makers in the village and by 1935, there were only five enterprises left: Walter Baker (the baker), Philip Baker (corn merchant), and shopkeepers, Reginald Collard, Philip Baker and William Trunks. Only two carpenters remained – Conrad George Reading (the Reading family had provided this service throughout the period and before), and Arthur Windo. The village still had a Sub Post Office run by the Stacey family at one of the Old Post Office Cottages. The period from 1883 to 1935 records a marginal decrease in the number of market gardeners to eight although this same period did see an increase in the number of farmers to 31.

LEATHER PRODUCTION

Leather production had been established in the parish by the 1630s. There was a tanner in the village in 1667 with tan-houses at Primmore by 1677 and another at Maunsel during the 18th century. Records show that a Simon Reepe from the parish was selling his wares as far afield at Saint Whites Fair, near Cricket St Thomas, between 1637 and 1649.

BRICKWORKS

Brickworks were recorded in the southern part of Petherton Park in 1670 and there were brickfields with three kilns near Hedging at Outwood in the early 1800s where clay was extracted for brick manufacture. The trade ceased in the 1870s, but is remembered by way of the naming of Brickyard Farm in Banklands.

WOODLANDS

Petherton Park was richly wooded and from the early 13th century grants of timber (mostly oak but also alder, maple, hazel and thorn) were regularly made for building work in the adjacent areas. The sale of timber provided a reliable and steady income which, in the late 16th century (1580), could be as much as £200 per annum. Wood was sold from North Moor and Newton Plecy in the 14th century but by the late 1600s many of the woods had been cleared for arable farming, meadow and pasture land. By the late 18th century the timber on the moors was said to no longer hold any value.

The Black Horse in Maunsel Road, which was demolished in the late 1970s. The girl in the tree is Terena McCullam (née Young).

Church Orchard, reputed to have been The Blue Lamb.

Chapter 3: Inns and Alehouses

There were unlicensed ale-sellers in the parish of North Petherton in the 14th century, some of whom would have lived in the village. In 1640, three alehouses were closed at Tuckerton, Primmore and North Moor, but several still remained in 1647. Even during the 18th century magistrates were concerned about unlicensed alehouses and drunkenness on or around May Day. In 1686, one or two inns in the village could provide 'three beds and stabling for three horses' and by 1688 there were three licensed victuallers here. One of them was probably at the Black Horse, recorded by name in 1711, and in business until the 1780s. A modern property called Tor View now occupies the site.

The Royal Oak, named in 1724, was certainly open between 1688 and 1779 but may have operated much later than this. It is shown on the Tithe Map of 1809 with a tenant named as Richard Atwell. In 1841 Robert Bell was the tenant. Another inn at Maunsel Road was the Rising Sun, now Dunns Cottage, where in 1841 Jane Bamfield was the landlady.

There were some unnamed beer and cider houses recorded in 1841, 1851 and 1872, including Church Orchard in Church Road which is reputed to have been a cider house known as The Blue Lamb.

An article in the *Bristol Evening Post* in 1951 suggested that there was also a public house called The Lamb in the village. The 1841 Tithe Map shows cider houses in West Newton, Tuckerton and in Maunsel Road, where Thomas Whitehead is shown as the tenant, but there is no later record of a public house in North Newton until the opening of The Harvest Moon in 1962.

From 1871, The Royal Oak at North Moor Corner existed as an inn until it closed in 1924. An early tithe map of 1809 showed that John Jeanes was the tenant and the 1891 census shows James Habberfield as a farmer and Innkeeper in North Moor.

Early in the 20th century, Starkeys, Knight and Ford, a local brewery, attempted to open a public house in the village. They purchased what is now known as Starkeys Cottage, the home of Gordon Finnimore, but were unable to obtain a licence and subsequently sold the property to Albert Broughton.

In the late 1950s from the 168 houses canvassed in the village, 350 inhabitants signed in favour of a new public house. Among the four objectors was the tenant of Penrod House, Mr Albert Lines, and the then owner, Mrs Coate. Eventually, the Bridgwater firm of Harris Bros & Collard built The Harvest Moon. Mr Harris had bought the land with planning permission for two houses. After the absence of any such establishment for a period of 100 years the village had a public house again. It was opened by Lady Freda Slade who drew the first pint and remarked 'there used to be three public houses in the village, but they were all closed because of the fighting!'

PUB REMINISCENCES

Stuart Scriven has fond memories of his life at The Moon. His father, Jack, was the first landlord and ran the pub until 1969 together with his wife, Vera, their children, David, Stuart, Elizabeth Ann, and her husband, Robert Vellacott.

Jack gave up farming in Wellington before becoming a landlord, but kept his hand in at the local markets during the week, buying and selling cattle and leaving the pub to Vera. At weekends it was all hands on deck and Stuart and David were even expected to wear white shirts and black bow ties – how times have changed! At the same time, they were also learning the meat trade and, once the pub was established, a restaurant area was made at the back of the lounge, the property extended and a kitchen built. Stuart's job on Mondays was to cut up the steaks (which he still does in his business in North Petherton, F. J. Scriven & Sons). By this time, he had started 'courting' Goody (Gwendolyn) White who was to become his wife and had her serving the meals while he was busy cooking in the kitchen!

Jack had a reputation for running a strict, tight ship and would not stand any nonsense, especially from the local lads. If they started to get a bit cheeky or noisy, he was not averse to turfing them out by the scruff of the neck – and as he was a large man, no-one argued with him. It was a regular occurrence for the Petherton boys to taunt the Newton boys at the school corner but, as Stuart recalls, the Newton boys always saw them off!

Lads at the time often visited the Green Dragon at Thurloxton which was a bit of a 'spit and sawdust' place. Among Stuart's friends were John Durbin, John Durman, Jim Miller and Steve Clatworthy and the whole group used to go about in John Durbin's Transit van. Once, when it was snowing and no vehicles could get out of the village, they used John Durman's tractor with a pallet attached to the back. Stuart often came home late after his parents had gone to bed and

Dunns Cottage, once the Rising Sun.

The Royal Oak at North Moor Corner before renovation in the late 1980s.

would stack up aluminium beer barrels and climb up to his sister's bedroom window to be let in. He also recalls his brother, David, going 'night fishing' with Les Farthing – an excuse to find the local girls (the Clatworthys were mentioned!). Jack had Harlequin Great Danes, a mynah bird and a South-African parrot called Charlie. Charlie could wolf whistle and often got Stuart into trouble with the ladies frequenting the pub. Spoofing (rounds of drinks) was a pastime on Sunday mornings, encouraged of course by Stuart and David. The most frequently involved were Leo Richards, Brian Williams and Gordon Collard.

During the early 1990s several landlords came and went and the Moon went through some ups and downs. Tony and Sue Hughes should certainly be mentioned, whose time at the pub is to be counted amongst the 'ups'. They came from

Cheddar and made a tremendous job of creating a friendly atmosphere with Sue's culinary skills well displayed in the kitchen. Alas, heavy rents forced them out of the business but they love Newton so much that they decided to stay in the area and are both members of the Village Hall Committee and active devotees of the local concert group.

The present landlord is Tony Smith who, with the help of Debbie, has maintained a high standard of service, and patrons old and new are paying regular visits.

Left and above: *Tony Smith and Debbie, mine hosts at the Harvest Moon.*

Below: *Opening of the Harvest Moon by Lady Freda Slade in September 1962. Left to right: G. Harris, B.W. Stone, F. J. Scriven, Lady Freda Slade, A.M.P. Luscombe, W. Foster and E. Harris.*

Above: *Court Farm.*

Below: *Coombe Cottage owes its name to a milkmaid called Annie Tucker who worked for a former owner of the property, Mr Tucker.*

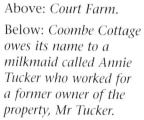

Above: *Brickyard farm, now renamed Cider Press Farm.*

Opposite page: *Bankland Farm from the air.*

Chapter 4: Around the Parish

BANKLAND

The area now known as Bankland was held by John Bluet in 1573, descending as part of North Petherton Manor until at least 1850. It is one of seven hamlets which, together with the village of North Newton, make up the parish (the others being Rydon, Chadmead, Bankland, Tuckerton, Hedging and Primmore). A capital messuage (a large residential property) recorded between 1573 and 1757 may have been Bankland Farm, which dates from the 16th century, 'with a three-roomed plan and cross passage'. The rear wing of the property was added in the 18th century when the house was re-roofed and re-fitted. The farm has been in the Habberfield family for many years.

Court Farm, now owned and occupied by John and Carol Habberfield, was originally part of one of the five estates called Newton (mentioned in the Domesday Book as being held by Ralph) which was later to become the Maunsel Estate. Marmaduke Ling bought the property in 1613 and it passed to his granddaughter, Eleanor Court, after which it became known as Court Farm. Jeremiah Dewdney bought it in 1759, selling it to William Webber in 1822. On his death it was left to his relations, the Jeanes family. John and Carol purchased the property in 1981. The original dwelling was constructed of wattle and daub with cob walls, some of which are still in evidence today. The house has been extended over the years using red bricks made locally in Bridgwater.

Brickyard Farm is situated opposite Court Farm and until recently was owned by John and Anne Guerin (née Jeanes) and family. It was built in the 1920s and John and Anne think that it owes its name to the fact that brick used for building or repairing the canal was said to have been stored there. However, another school of thought suggests that it derived its name from the brickworks which were at nearby Outwood until the late 19th century. The farmhouse was sold in the summer of 1999 and has been renamed Cider Press Farm. The Guerin family is taking the original name to their new property situated next to Court Farm. Anne has, therefore, not ventured far from her childhood home!

Coombe Cottage is owned by Alan and Wendy Darch. This thatched property which is rumoured to be over 300 years old, was previously known as 'Sunnybanks', the name having been changed in 1970 when it was owned by a builder named Mr Smith. At the time it was uninhabitable because it was used as an animal feedstore by the previous owner, a Mr Tucker.

WEST NEWTON

Previously known as Newton Comitis and Newton Hawys, the name of West Newton was not used until the late 14th century. West Newton's history dates back to the pre-Domesday era. Prior to the Norman Conquest it was also called Newentone and was held by a wealthy Saxon, Lewin, who owned, among other properties, manors at Combwich and Minehed. William granted West Newton to one of his most powerful knights, Eustace, Count of Boulogne and it is from this gentleman that the name Newton Comitis or 'Count's Newton' derived. The manor was held by descendants of Eustace until 1159, when, on the death of William, son of Stephen, King of England, it merged with the crown under

West Newton Manor.

King Henry II. The manor and estate have been divided between several families over the years.

By the mid 13th century it was held by the de Newton family. By 1385, Alice, wife of John Copplestone, a Devon lawyer and politician, held the entire manor which then remained in the ownership of the Copplestone family until the end of the 15th century. It passed briefly into the control of the Sydenham family via Catherine Copplestone who was married to John Sydenham and on Catherine's death in 1524, the estate was split among her three sisters and subsequently divided into six parts. The story from this point becomes complex and is beyond the scope of this book, but suffice to say that there was a succession of acrimonious lawsuits over claims for the estate by members of the sisters' families.

Whilst the various claimants were pursuing their grievances, the Chick or Cheeke family of North Petherton began to cast covetous eyes on the evidently neglected manor of West Newton. From 1580, the Cheekes started to buy shares and they certainly made dramatic progress; within just two years George Cheeke was the wealthiest inhabitant of West Newton! And by 1630, at the time of his death, George's grandson, Henry, held five-sixths of the manor. The death of Henry's son (yet another Henry) brought an end to the Cheeke connection as he died without male issue. In 1668 Henry's daughter, Dorothy, married for the second time. Her spouse happened to be the remaining shareholder, Sir Edward Phelip of Montacute who was considered to be 'a good catch'. This meant that the manor descended with Montacute Manor until 1810 when it was sold at auction at the George Inn, Bridgwater, for some £18 000 to Thomas Warre, a member both of the Diplomatic Corps and of the Warre family from nearby Hestercombe House. The manor remained with the family until Mary Elliott, the last owner and the niece of John Henry Warre, sold it in 1904 for £7500 to the tenant, William Hellier-Smith (who had taken over the property in 1882). The Hellier-Smiths farmed the estate until 1939, when William's widow sold it to Mrs W. Hampton for some £9000.

In 1958 the farm was bought by Showerings of Shepton Mallet. It has subsequently been sold and many of the outbuildings converted by their new owners into homes. Today the manor house itself is occupied by Roger and Ann Goodwin.

The house was formerly called Courthouse but is now referred to simply as 'The Manor'. It may date from the 14th century and is probably built on the site of a Saxon hall. The 1891 census shows the occupier as William H. Smith, the farm being of some 270 acres. In his *History of Somerset*, the historian, Collinson, writes that there was a chapel at West Newton which was given to the monastery of Buckland in Durston by its founder, William de Erleigh. There was also a school in the hamlet until the late 18th century (see Education).

West Newton Farm probably dates from the 1700s. In 1841 it had a wagon house, linhay (cowshed) and cider house, which were replaced in c.1870 by stables, a chaff house and engine house. The present owners are Dennis and Heather Hill.

CHADMEAD

Chadmead Manor was also known as Brickland, or Bankland Chadmead. Like most of the hamlets in the parish, over the years it has been held by several families whose names will be familiar to those from the locality. In 1298, Henry of Somerset held Chadmead and by 1485 it was part of the Bluets' Manor of North Petherton. It was sold in 1498 to George Sydenham and passed, via the granddaughter of Sylvester Sydenham, into the hands of the Rogers family of Cannington. In 1672, it passed to Hugh Roger's grandson, Alexander Popham of Littlecote in Wiltshire.

Annie Boyer feeding the poultry at Eames Farm c.1900.

Alexander died without male issue in 1705 and by 1712 the manor had reverted to Sir Copplestone Warwick Bampfylde, heir of Warwick Bampfylde and nephew of Henry Rogers. In 1720, Sir Copplestone sold the manor to Sir Thomas Wroth. It then descended with the Wroth estate in Lyng until the death of Elizabeth Acland in 1806, when her daughter, Elizabeth, and her son, Wroth Palmer Acland, held it. In 1815 part of the property was put up for sale and in 1829 the portion known as Little Bankland was sold to Sir John Slade. John Acland's son, Perigrine, retained the remainder of the estate called 'Eames' in 1838 as part of Buckland Sororum Manor.

In 1423, a house existed on the estate. The capital messuage was called Chadmead or Eames, the name deriving from a former tenant, a John Eams, who was known to be living in the parish in 1647. In 1754, Arthur Acland reserved the right to hold courts in the house but in 1767 the house was described as 'unfinished' with the barns and offices in ruins. By 1771, the house had fallen into decay and had been demolished.

The present-day Eames Farm could have been built on the site of Eames. By the mid 1800s the farm was owned by the Portman Estate and tenanted by John Boyer (the present owner's great-grandfather). In the 1930s, Metford Boyer bought the farm from the Portman Estate and in 1973 sold it to his grandson, John, and his wife, Margaret.

The 1770 map shows that there were at least 19 dwellings in Chadmead. Amongst the many interesting properties are: Big Bere Farm, formerly the home of Francis George Duddridge and now owned by Terry and Sarah Wolfe; Chadmead Farmhouse, the main part of which is thought to have been built in the 16th century and is now owned by Paula Darnell; and Royal Oak, which is the site of the old public house, presently being renovated by Ian and Jennifer Duddridge.

RYDON

In the early 16th century, Rydon was owned by Margery Lyte who may have been a member of the Lyte family of Lytes Cary, Charlton Mackerell. In 1561, Margery's son, John, sold the property to Nicholas Haswell (of Haswell House in Goatshurst) and he subsequently conveyed it to John Phelps in 1620. In 1685, John's son sold it to Andrew Moore (a descendent of Thomas Moore), a Bridgwater merchant who enlarged the estate and was later succeeded by his nephew, another Andrew Moore. Andrew's son, William, died in 1768, and the property passed to his widow. She remarried and in 1792 settled Rydon on William's nephew, Hill Dawe (from Ditcheat). The Moore tomb can be

Right: Tomb of Andrew Moore in St Peters, dated 1616.

seen on the left of the entrance path to the church of St Peters in North Newton village.

In 1826, the Revd Thomas Coney bought Rydon. Lower Rydon Farm (which is thought to be 16th century or earlier) is now occupied by Jeffrey Duddridge who for many years lived there with his late wife, Edna. It is possible that the fireplace came from the Old Priory at Buckland. The duck shed is a good example of a medieval-style building.

Long Orchard after and (inset) *during conversion.*

Tuckerton Grange

Tuckerton Farm c.1900 – the site of the hospital of Buckland Priory for the aged, sick and infirm.

TUCKERTON

Tuckerton is mentioned in the Domesday Book but there was a settlement on the site before this as it had been held by a Saxon thane, Elaf, before 1066. After 1066 it was held by Ralph for Roger of Courseulles, who added it to his other 90 estates. In 1066 the estate was valued at 20 shillings, but by the time Roger acquired it its value had halved. The estate passed from Roger into the hands of another family of great landowners, the de Columbers, who were lords of Nether Stowey Manor, and although Tuckerton was recorded as Tokar Newton in the 13th century (suggesting that it was part of Newton), it was held by Nether Stowey in the 1200s and 1300s.

In the early 13th century, land from Tuckerton was given to the Hospitallers of Buckland. They eventually received the entire hamlet, holding Tuckerton until 1428 or possibly until the Dissolution of the Monasteries. They set up a small hospital on the site now occupied by Tuckerton Farm.

After the Dissolution, Tuckerton is thought to have been granted to William Portman and Alexander Popham. The manor at Tuckerton stayed in the Popham family until 1628 when it passed to the Crown as a result of the outlawing of Edward Popham for debt. From this time ownership follows the familiar pattern of passing down through several families.

In 1671, Tuckerton was owned by Robert Hunt, passing to John Jeanes in 1703 and, by 1791, to Sir John Durbin from Bristol who acquired the estate possibly through marriage. In 1839, his son, Joseph Jeanes Durbin, sold to Sir John Slade. The estate then descended with Maunsel until at least 1870. In 1851 Tuckerton Farm was sold to the Portman family who, in the early 1900s, sold it to their tenant, Walter Day. The farm remained in the Day family until 1988, when the property and land was auctioned and the barns and outbuildings converted into residences.

The farmhouse is now occupied by the Evans family and one of the barn conversions – Long Orchard House – is occupied by the Lowndes family. They bought the barn (which is thought to be over 150 years old) in 1991 and converted it into the property we see today. The hayloft became the guest-room, the cider-making area the master bedroom, the cattle byre the lounge, and the coach house the dining room.

The other conversions include: Days Granary, owned by Tony Fulker and Jane Light, The Old Wagon House, owned by Peter and Mary Ashton, and Tuckerton Grange, owned by Brian and Denise Herrick.

Other properties in Tuckerton include: Nutley Cottage, owned by Andrew and Cherry Green, Musgraves, which Mr and Mrs Tipper have recently purchased (and from where, in the early 1900s, a Mrs Crewe used to hire out carriages), Horseshoe Cottage, built since 1980 and owned by Douglas and June Shopland, The Corner House, The Red House and The Stables.

HEDGING

By the late 13th century, Hedging belonged to Buckland Priory but after the Dissolution it appears to have been granted to the Sydenham family. In 1706 Sir Phillip Sydenham sold a house and approximately 40 acres at Hedging to Giles Gardiner. It subsequently passed from families called Selleck, Combes and Cole, the latter owning all of Hedging by 1858.

Hedging Barton, presently owned by Mrs Gillian Richards, was originally a two-roomed medieval house with a cross passage, a third room having been added in the 1600s. In its time, it has been a farm and, according to the present owners, a wheelwright's shop. In the 1970s, pottery found in the grounds was authenticated by the County Museum as being of Roman origin and helped confirm beliefs that there had been a Roman dwelling on the site. Across the road from Hedging Barton are the ruins (which are difficult to distinguish) of two cottages. One is said to have been a blacksmith's shop.

Hedging Farm (*opposite*), owned by Alan and Diane Coram, is reputed to be the oldest property in the hamlet. During the conversion of one of the outbuildings (now called Barnfields and occupied by Robert and Dawn Coram), artifacts were found which suggest it was once owned by Buckland Priory.

The 1891 census showed that James Bradford and his son Robert were blacksmiths and although *Kelly's Directories* for 1883 and 1889 list Robert Kearle as a blacksmith, by the time of the entry for 1894, he is shown as a carpenter. The 1889 list also shows that a veterinary surgeon called James Bond resided in Hedging – and another vet called Bond is thought to have been in residence at Hedging House in the 1920s and '30s. This is now owned by Frederick Partridge.

The 1894 and 1897 lists show a George Bond in business as a farrier. However, the lists for 1902 and 1906 show that the farrier was then one James Bond. There were no more entries in later lists.

Carol Habberfield's grandparents used to run a shop from Dawes Cottage in the early 1900s and her mother, Edna Duddridge, was born at Dawes in 1920 and lived there until 1938. The cottage is now owned by Donald and Irene Kean

Below and left: *Edna Duddridge as a baby with her mother in the court-yard of Dawes Cottage 1922 and Edna, aged two, in the same spot.*

Opposite page: *Diane Coram and her two granddaughters at Hedging Farm.*

(Donald looks after the nearby St Michaels Church), but Edna has many memories of her time there. Hedging was, she remembers, then quite a busy place. Her mother sold sweets, tobacco and cigarettes and supplies for the shop were brought in from the wholesalers in Bridgwater by horse and cart. The cottage was a farm workers' cottage for nearby Dawes Farm (which is now called Hedging Farm) and Edna's father, Harold Bennett, worked there after the First World War for Mr Godfrey. Groceries and meat were delivered twice a week and bread delivered daily, all by horse and cart.

Opposite Edna's home was Drakes the farrier's, where the children watched the horses being shod. Edna also remembered that there were always cows being driven past the house on their way to Starsland Farm for servicing by the bull owned by Mr Roberts, and a constant 'traffic' as cream, butter, eggs and cider were taken to market from the farm. Durston Station (*see page 6*) was also very busy. From here sheep were transported to and from the markets and coal and other necessities were supplied to the hamlet. Several of the inhabitants were employed at the station, including Mr Ingram and Mr Warren who were both from Hedging Lane.

Edna remembered that the District Nurse was Nurse Ratty from North Petherton and that she was very strict! Edna used to walk to school in North Newton, but had no wellington boots and the lanes were not covered in tarmac in those days. If she heard the school bell and had not yet passed Maunsel House she knew that the time had come to run!

People worked very hard and often used footpaths to walk many miles to work. Harry Woollen from Willow Cottage, for example, sometimes walked to Highbridge for a day's thrashing. Hedging was also home to market gardeners like the Vearncombes of Barn Cottage and the Williams family of Hedging Barton, where there was a fish pond. Mrs Pine of Hedging Lane took in sewing and was a herbalist and, if you could afford it, a horse and governess cart could be hired from Mrs Crewe at Musgraves.

The chapel had a regular congregation of about 40 with a Sunday School in the charge of Mr Pike of Willow Barton, who, being the Station Master at Washford, was away for most of the week. Edna could remember sleeping at Willow Barton during the week as company for Mr Pike's housekeeper, Mrs Adams, as she didn't like to stay in the house on her own.

Chapel Cottage is now occupied by June and Michael Snellgrove and Orchard Cottage by Lily Taylor, Orchard End by the Wooldridge family, and Orchard View by Margaret Sutcliffe.

Hedging House

Hedging Barton

PRIMMORE

Primmore once belonged to the Hospitallers at Buckland. After the Dissolution of the Monasteries it was held by Thomas Musgrave and is unusual in that it appears to have stayed with the same family for many years. The Musgrave family control ended in 1800 and in 1838, the owner was William Beadon.

Sylvia Hillman, who owns Stonecroft, remembers when her father ran a butcher's shop from his farm at Primore before the war and when the Willows, now owned by Arthur Davis, was a cobbler's. John and Jean Nation own Primore Cottage, Roger and Ann Warren own Bramble Cottage and Daniel and Sarah Anholt own Primmore Farm.

Chapter 5: St Michaelchurch

The tiny parish of St Michaelchurch covers just 46 acres and probably originated in the 11th century. A road from North Moor to Chadmead was recorded on its eastern boundary in 1401, but fell out of use when the Bridgwater to Taunton Canal was cut through it in the 1820s. Although no woods were recorded in 1086, field names like 'Woodcroft' and 'Hamwood' would indicate that at some time the parish was planted with trees. By 1839 some land on the eastern side was used to form Maunsel Park and two cottages were used as staff cottages.

The Manor of St Michaelchurch was probably an estate with tenant farmers, as no capital messuage has been traced. In 1066 it was held by Alwi and by 1086 by Ansger 'the cook' (as listed in the Domesday Book). By the 13th century it came into the possession of the Erleigh family who had estates near Reading and who held it until around 1373. From 1377/8 to around 1425 the estate was under the control of the Cheddar family of Bristol. In 1425 it was conveyed to the Seymour family, passing to Sir Thomas Seymour in 1457. It remained under the control of the Seymours until 1779, when Henry Seymour and his son conveyed it to John Slade of Maunsel in North Petherton. By then the Seymours' estates had shrunk from the 125 acres held in several parishes during the 14th and 15th centuries to just 26 acres of land within St Michaelchurch.

There were several other small estates in the parish. One, called 'Elerhaye', belonged to Newton Plecy Chantry from the late 13th century. This estate eventually descended with the Bluets' North Petherton Manor to the Slade family. In the 13th century Henry of Erleigh gave land to Philip Maunsel and a small estate to John Wyter. The Maunsel estate was probably on the north side of Maunsel House to the east of the parish and descended with the Manor of Maunsel in North Petherton. In 1417 the Maunsels acquired the Wyters' land.

LOCAL ECONOMY

It would appear that over the years the size of the parish has decreased. In 1086, one ploughland was recorded and it was taxed on half a hide (60 acres). During the Middle Ages the manor included land in neighbouring parishes and in 1377 had four stalls in Taunton Market. By the 17th century, farming was mainly arable, producing wheat, barley and beans and there were 14 or 15 holdings recorded in the parish (though none of them were large). In the 18th century, houses were let with between two and thirteen acres. In 1823 there were nine dwellings in the parish and by 1839 there were five smallholdings and the mill. For the rest of the century, the Mill House, Maunsel Lodge and three other houses made up the parish.

The principal house was Michael Church Farm, although most of the 200 acreas (providing employment for six labourers) lay outside the farm. The farmhouse fell into disuse in the middle of the 20th century and was demolished around 1955, although the remains of some of the outbuildings are still visible. The main building was thatched and the last farmer is said to have been J. Habberfield. Plans have now been drawn up to build a house on the site.

*View of St Michaelchurch showing the church with the farm ruins beyond, the mill house,
Mill Cottage and Maunsel House in the background.*

Top: *remains of Michael Church Farm, soon to be a barn conversion.*

Above: *Keepers Cottage, formerly the home of the Lewis family.*

Left: *The Mill House after renovation.*

TRADE AND GOVERNMENT

Serge weaving may have taken place in the 17th century and there was certainly a family of tanners and a carpenter in the 18th century. The tanning office was used as a school in the late 18th century and is thought to have been run by Mrs Slade. In the 19th century there was a carpenter, butcher, mason, dressmaker, market gardener and miller in the parish.

A watermill was given to Philip Maunsell by Henry of Erleigh in the late 13th century and this mill, usually known as 'Maunsel Mill', descended with the Maunsel family in North Petherton and formed part of Maunsel House when it was rebuilt in the early 1700s. In addition there was also another mill in St Michaelchurch which closed around 1930 (see Trade and Industry).

Manor courts were held in the parish. They were held twice a year in 1632 and were still being held in the early 17th century. Two churchwardens were recorded in the late 16th and 17th centuries and in the 1700s there was a churchwarden and a sidesman. There may have been a vestry in the 19th century. The parish became part of Bridgwater Rural District in 1894 and in 1974 formed part of Sedgemoor District. It is now the smallest parish in Somerset.

THE PEOPLE OF ST MICHAELCHURCH

An article in the *Bridgwater Mercury* in June 1984 recounts the memories of the parish's Lewis and Vickery families. The Lewis family lived in Keepers Cottage and Mrs Lewis was the then churchwarden of St Michaelchurch, having lived in the parish for 38 years. She could remember when the population was a 'bustling' 27 (compared with just 9 at the time of the interview).

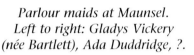

Parlour maids at Maunsel.
Left to right: Gladys Vickery
(née Bartlett), Ada Duddridge, ?.

The Vickery family lived in the front lodge of Maunsel House. Tom Vickery was a retired coach and lorry driver, but had once worked as a groom at the big house. He remembered the days when the Grange was busy with workers and he toiled seven days a week for a pound. His wife Gladys had also been employed in the house, working as a parlour maid from the age of 14 until she married. Dr Jeremy Budd and his wife Charlotte occupied the remaining house, Mill Cottage.

In 1639 there were said to be 14 or 15 'ancient inhabited tenements besides cottages' in the parish (the sites of which are now, unfortunately, unknown). Since the 18th century the number of dwellings has declined. Four, for example, were demolished in the 1820s and '30s. In 1801 the population was 41 and by 1851 this had risen to 50. However, within a decade this had dropped by over 30 per cent to 32. The population barely changed until 1901 when it was around 30, but by 1931 it had fallen to 24 and was down to just 9 in 1984.

MAUNSEL HOUSE

Since 1771 Maunsel House has been in the possession of the Slade family and, during much of this time, the building was left to fall into a considerable state of disrepair. However, all was not lost, for the present owner, Sir Benjamin Slade Bt., set to work to return both the house and the estate to a somewhat more befitting condition. When first opened to the public by Sir Benjamin at 50 pence per visit, Maunsel was unique in the sight it offered to the public. In 1986, an article in the *Western Daily Press* described it thus:

... [as] having what estate agents refer to as potential. No red ropes separate you from the things you can't touch as you wander around. No family portraits glare down at you from the walls. Your eye is more likely to be caught by the hand-written signs on the doors, 'ONLY FOUR ON THE STAIRS: FLOOR UNSAFE' – or drawn irresistibly to the stains and holes that mark the passage of rain water from the roof to the ground floor.

Today the story is somewhat different, much toil and an estimated £1 million having gone a long way to returning the house to a more deserved state. Weddings and receptions are held there, and Sir Benjamin's weekend sojourns ensure that Maunsel retains a lived-in atmosphere.

The date of the foundation of the house is unknown, but an estate known as 'Maunsel Manor' dating back at least as far as 1086 has been identified. This was held by Roger Arundel, a Norman baron who forcibly removed the previous lord, Brictwold, an Anglo-Saxon landowner, who is recorded in 1066 as holding an estate called Newton. At the time, the estate comprised 30 acres of woodland, the total being valued at five shillings.

By the 12th century the estate was owned by William de Erleigh from North Petherton and was subsequently given to Philip Arbalistarious (a cross-bow man) in free marriage (i.e. with no dowry) to Mabel, his daughter, for the yearly rent of two pigs. William's widow, Aziria, confirmed the grant for Philip's son, another Philip, now called de Maunsel (a name which is believed to derive from 'la manche', meaning a sleeve of land).

The ensuing Maunsel family made few advantageous marriages with wealthy heiresses. There is occasional word of a marriage into the Bournvilles of Dillington, the Colstons of Bristol and the Kings of Bedminster, but these marriages brought little money into the estate. Whilst none of the family served as Sheriff of Somerset, one member, John,

Maunsel House and part of the surrounding parkland.

Horse and carriage from Maunsel House with Mr Biddulph the coachman.

Staff at Maunsel House in the mid 1920s. Miss Jemmett Brown is sitting in the front.

THE PEOPLE OF ST MICHAELCHURCH

An article in the *Bridgwater Mercury* in June 1984 recounts the memories of the parish's Lewis and Vickery families. The Lewis family lived in Keepers Cottage and Mrs Lewis was the then churchwarden of St Michaelchurch, having lived in the parish for 38 years. She could remember when the population was a 'bustling' 27 (compared with just 9 at the time of the interview).

The Vickery family lived in the front lodge of Maunsel House. Tom Vickery was a retired coach and lorry driver, but had once worked as a groom at the big house. He remembered the days when the Grange was busy with workers and he toiled seven days a week for a pound. His wife Gladys had also been employed in the house, working as a parlour maid from the age of 14 until she married. Dr Jeremy Budd and his wife Charlotte occupied the remaining house, Mill Cottage.

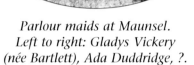

Parlour maids at Maunsel.
Left to right: Gladys Vickery
(née Bartlett), Ada Duddridge, ?.

In 1639 there were said to be 14 or 15 'ancient inhabited tenements besides cottages' in the parish (the sites of which are now, unfortunately, unknown). Since the 18th century the number of dwellings has declined. Four, for example, were demolished in the 1820s and '30s. In 1801 the population was 41 and by 1851 this had risen to 50. However, within a decade this had dropped by over 30 per cent to 32. The population barely changed until 1901 when it was around 30, but by 1931 it had fallen to 24 and was down to just 9 in 1984.

MAUNSEL HOUSE

Since 1771 Maunsel House has been in the possession of the Slade family and, during much of this time, the building was left to fall into a considerable state of disrepair. However, all was not lost, for the present owner, Sir Benjamin Slade Bt., set to work to return both the house and the estate to a somewhat more befitting condition. When first opened to the public by Sir Benjamin at 50 pence per visit, Maunsel was unique in the sight it offered to the public. In 1986, an article in the *Western Daily Press* described it thus:

... [as] having what estate agents refer to as potential. No red ropes separate you from the things you can't touch as you wander around. No family portraits glare down at you from the walls. Your eye is more likely to be caught by the hand-written signs on the doors, 'ONLY FOUR ON THE STAIRS: FLOOR UNSAFE' – or drawn irresistibly to the stains and holes that mark the passage of rain water from the roof to the ground floor.

Today the story is somewhat different, much toil and an estimated £1 million having gone a long way to returning the house to a more deserved state. Weddings and receptions are held there, and Sir Benjamin's weekend sojourns ensure that Maunsel retains a lived-in atmosphere.

The date of the foundation of the house is unknown, but an estate known as 'Maunsel Manor' dating back at least as far as 1086 has been identified. This was held by Roger Arundel, a Norman baron who forcibly removed the previous lord, Brictwold, an Anglo-Saxon landowner, who is recorded in 1066 as holding an estate called Newton. At the time, the estate comprised 30 acres of woodland, the total being valued at five shillings.

By the 12th century the estate was owned by William de Erleigh from North Petherton and was subsequently given to Philip Arbalistarious (a cross-bow man) in free marriage (i.e. with no dowry) to Mabel, his daughter, for the yearly rent of two pigs. William's widow, Aziria, confirmed the grant for Philip's son, another Philip, now called de Maunsel (a name which is believed to derive from 'la manche', meaning a sleeve of land).

The ensuing Maunsel family made few advantageous marriages with wealthy heiresses. There is occasional word of a marriage into the Bournvilles of Dillington, the Colstons of Bristol and the Kings of Bedminster, but these marriages brought little money into the estate. Whilst none of the family served as Sheriff of Somerset, one member, John,

Maunsel House and part of the surrounding parkland.

Horse and carriage from Maunsel House with Mr Biddulph the coachman.

Staff at Maunsel House in the mid 1920s. Miss Jemmett Brown is sitting in the front.

did serve two terms, in 1449 and 1454, as a Member of Parliament for Bridgwater.

In 1544, with several extensions having been built onto the original building, Maunsel House was recorded as 'Maunsel Place'. In 1631 Richard de Maunsel's widow, Elizabeth, and his heir, John, sold the estate to John Harvey, who in turn sold it to William Bacon of Broomfield in 1648. Thomas Bacon, William's grandson, died in 1722 leaving four daughters who, in 1727, sold their shares to Henry Portman. In the same year Thomas' nephew, Sir Edward Seymour, conveyed the estate to his son, Alexander, upon whose death in 1733, the estate passed to his sister, Letitia, for life and then to her son Alexander Seymour Gapper.

Gapper mortgaged the estate heavily and left it to a friend, John Nichols, who passed it on to his two sons. By 1769, the mortgage debt amounted to £4815.9s. and exceeded the value of the house and the estate.

In 1772 the property was sold to John Slade of Hammersmith, London. He had been born in Burstock, Dorset, and was one of the commissioners of the Victual Licensing Board for the Royal Navy. He had previously bought North Petherton Manor in 1768. Under John Slade the estate expanded and records show that it included the whole of Coxhill, the house and immediate land of Big Bere Farmhouse, land on both sides of the

Above: *Repairs to the house well under way.*
Below: *Maunsel House restored to its former glory, now the home of Sir Benjamin Slade.*

canal from Coxhill to the Maunsel lock, and the bridge on the Outwood Road. The estate bordered on the hamlets of Tuckerton and West Newton. In common with many of the previous owners, John Slade added onto the house. However, it should be noted that one of the unique and much-treasured qualities of Maunsel is that none of these alterations has 'modernised' the property or covered up what was already in place.

In Tudor times, a hall and first-floor chamber were added and the medieval hall became the kitchen and scullery. A brick oven from the time can still be seen on a windowsill. In the 16th century, a Tudor ceiling was added together with panelling in the first-floor rooms. The ensuing centuries saw the addition of more rooms, including a drawing room, which features Regency plaster moulding. John Slade refitted several rooms, rebuilt the staircase and erected the Athelney Monument to mark the site of the Athelney Abbey to which Alfred the Great retreated in 877. He also bequeathed the sum of 40 shillings to be paid annually for ever, to purchase tools of husbandry for the use of the labouring poor of the parish.

His son, another John, who had a successful and colourful military career, succeeded him in 1801. He rose to the rank of General in the 5th Regiment of Dragoon Guards and was decorated for gallantry on several occasions. During the

Peninsular Wars, two of his horses were shot from underneath him! He served under Wellington from 1809 to 1813 as Commander of a cavalry brigade and was created Baronet in 1831. With the assistance of architect, Richard Carver, extensive alterations were carried out to the house, which included the removal of the great chimney stack from the hall, the addition of the dining room and extension of the great hall to the north.

The second Sir Frederick William Slade appointed John Winter as tenant at Maunsel and in 1880 his son installed the billiard and library rooms. The estate then passed to Sir William Frederick Adolphus Slade who served in the Crimean War and the Indian Mutiny. Maunsel then passed to his son, Sir Cuthbert, and in turn, to his son, Sir Alfred. It was at this time that Mrs Louise Earl and Miss Jemmett Brown arrived as tenant managers and acted as benefactors to many in the village, holding annual Christmas and New Year parties for members of the Church Sunday School and their families.

As the house has stood the test of time and alterations have been made, so the area around the house has also been somewhat altered. By the early 18th century it included a dove-house, stables, barns, gardens, orchards and a large fishpond with an island. A moat was constructed in the early part of the century, possibly from earlier fishponds. The lodge, which incorporates a semi-circular thatched roof on the south side, is called 'The Dairy' and was built on the site of a former mill, probably in the late 18th or early 19th century. The northern lodge was rebuilt in the early 20th century. The park to the north of the house was established around 1828 when the north drive was made, hedges removed and a ha-ha reconstructed. James Veitch of Exeter supplied the ornamental trees for the planting along the north drive, around the moat and in a copse to the east of the house. A partly walled kitchen garden lay on the west side.

Unfortunately, under Sir Alfred, the estate went into decline with parts being sold off and trees felled and sold. During the Second World War the estate was used as a transit camp by both the British and American forces and by the time of Sir Alfred's death in 1960, much of the family fortune had gone. A large amount of the land had been lost and the house was in a sorry state of neglect. The title passed to Sir Alfred's brother, Sir Michael Nial Slade, the 6th Baronet, who died in 1962.

The house and what remained of the estate were sold to Cecil Mitford Slade, a member of another branch of the Slade family (originating from Sir John Slade's second marriage). Sir Alfred's widow, Lady Freda, continued to live in the house, paying a token rent. A well-known, charismatic lady, she was recalled in the *Western Daily Press* (1986) as having taken 'great delight' in 'exercising the family right to gallop along the canal towpath, jumping bicycles placed in her path by irate anglers with shouts of 'I'm a Slade!'

In 1974 Sir Michael's son, Sir Benjamin Slade, the 7th Baronet, bought a cottage and a third of an acre of land on the former Maunsel estate and set to work returning the estate to its former glory. In 1978 he bought back the house, with his Aunt Freda as a sitting tenant, and 12 remaining acres. The house cost £25 000 and he was advised that it would cost another £100 000 to carry out the necessary repairs. In 1982 he bought the 90-acre parkland and, to date, his holdings have increased to more than 700 acres. In 1986 Sir Benjamin announced a £470 000 renovation scheme and opened the house to visitors for a charge of 50 pence. From this modest start, he has rebuilt and, to a great extent, fulfilled the potential offered by Maunsel House and its estate.

Top: *Lady Freda Slade celebrating her birthday, 4 September 1980.*

Left: *Sir Benjamin Slade.*

Chapter 6: Farms and Farming

IN THE BEGINNING

Farming has been a main source of employment in the area for over 1000 years, the Romans and Celts being among the earliest farmers here. In 1066 there were five manors in North Newton covering an area of nine-and-a-half ploughlands. (A ploughland was defined as the amount of potential arable land on an estate expressed as a tax assessment, which varied according to regional conditions and class of soil.). Three of these ploughlands were 'demesne' which was land devoted to the lord's profit, whether a manor's land in its entirety, or a portion of land within a manor, worked by peasants as part of their obligations.

By 1274, the estate of William de Plessis extended over 168 acres of demesne. An acre was defined in those days as a day's ploughing for one plough team. This land was mainly arable and worth the grand total of £3.4s.6d.

In the early 14th century, wheat, barley and oats were the chief crops being grown at Newton Plecy, although the estate also sold hay, pasture and wood. By 1360, the 40 acres of demesne were let, the rents forming more than three-quarters of the total manorial income and by the middle of the 15th century the same estate was let entirely. At the same time, the income of the estate at Chadmead also came from rents and court profits.

Over the next four centuries, the structure of land and property changed dramatically. The 16th century saw Petherton (Newton) Park receiving about £150 a year from sales of wood and pasture. Towards the end of the century, the park was enclosed and let, increasing the income by more than 100 per cent to £380 per annum.

Bill Jeanes and Smart at Court Farm, 1950s.

By 1655, the park was divided into 11 holdings increasing to 15 by 1676. The rental income now stood at £889. After the death of Sir Thomas Wroth in 1724, several of these holdings were amalgamated to create four principal farms; Petherton Park, Parker's Field, Fordgate and Impens. The sale particulars for all four farms in 1833 stated that the combined rents for 1830 had been around £3000 per annum.

The details of the sale also mention that a man called Roger Carter was a tenant at Impens, paying £665 per annum in rent for 340 acres. The 1841 census shows that he was a married 50-year-old yeoman, with six children and two servants. The *Victorian History of Somerset* tells us that by 1851, Henry Parramore was renting all the four farms of Petherton Park. *Kelly's Directory* lists as tenant from 1883 to 1910 one James Q. Carter who we know, from the 1891 census, was then 39 years old, born in Middlesex, either unmarried or widowed and with a house-keeper, Mary Williams, and a servant, Avril Foster from North Petherton. All of the directories from 1914 to 1935 list Albert Broughton as the owner. Albert came from a farming family in North Perrott and as well as being a farmer he also served on the Board of Governors at the local school and was a local councillor. He was succeeded by his son, Geoffrey, who now leaves the running of the farm to his own son, James. For many years, Impens provided a pre-college training course for entrants to agricultural colleges such as Cirencester.

Another large property worthy of note is Great House, Brook Street. It was built by Sir Thomas Wroth and its fine quality is an indication of the agricultural prosperity once enjoyed within the parish. From 1660, the Wroths encouraged experimentation in agricultural techniques to increase productivity and profits. For example, two tenants were encouraged to test soap ashes instead of lime, others were directed to plant withies by meadow ditches, and earth and sand were used as dressing on wet land.

Mixed farming continued into the 18th century, including the raising of cattle, sheep and horses (mostly on the moors), and the growing of wheat, beans, oats and potatoes. After the enclosure of Northmoor, the cultivation of withies became a commercial prospect.

Although attempts had been made during the 13th century to drain and enclose small areas of North Moor, most of the land remained subject to common rights for pasture and fuel and people were encouraged to enhance drainage with man-made ditches. From the 1600s willow trees were planted along these ditches, leading to the growth in the willow industry. The commoners were responsible for the upkeep of the main drains or brooks around the edge of the moor and, in return, had rights known as 'ox-shoots' which entitled them to 'pasture one horse, two oxen, three yearlings, or ten sheep'.

CROPS

Facts and figures tell us much about the state of farming in the parish over the last 200 years:

1821: 66 per cent of families in the parish were employed in agriculture.

1838: 50 per cent of the land was used for arable farming.

1851: Henry Parramore employed at least 59 labourers, 2 master dairymen and 2 dairymaids.

1851: West Newton Farm was employing 14 labourers

1871: This had decreased to 4 men, 3 boys and 2 women. Benjamin Turner was tenant.

1881: The number stood at only 9. By this time, a number of market gardeners were in business and the 1891 census lists the following: Walter Adams (Brook Street), James Jeanes, Emily Reading and Stephen Clatworthy (Petherton Road), George Day, William Bond, and Alfred Lang (Church Road). There was one other in Hedging, name unknown.

1906: There were 11 market gardeners in the area, including Tuckerton.

Tuckerton Farm c.1900.

MARKET GARDENERS

The late Molly Sellick (whose family run a market-garden business from Burnt House Farm in Petherton Road), wrote in a scrapbook which, in 1965, was produced by the North Newton branch of the Women's Institute. Her article is called 'A Year in the Life of a Market Gardener' and includes the following:

Crops are harvested throughout the year. The land is so rich and fertile, that no sooner is one crop finishing, than another can be planted. From Christmas to March fresh vegetables such as turnips, swedes, parsnips, sprouts and cabbage are cut daily. While potatoes, carrots and beetroot are brought from their storage 'clamps'.

March until June, cauliflower, spring cabbage and lettuce are harvested. The really busy season is from June until August. New potatoes, carrots, spring onions, tomatoes, broad beans, runner beans, marrows, lettuce and peas are harvested. Many of these crops such as peas and potatoes are grown by the acre and outside help from 'travellers' is needed to gather the harvest. Pea picking commences in June and continues until September, by which time potato picking begins in earnest and continues until October/November. In addition to all this activity, during the summer months, strawberries, raspberries, gooseberries, blackcurrants and plums were picked and sent to the shops or turned into homemade jam.

Work went on and still does throughout the daylight hours to ensure that fresh produce is delivered to the consumer.

In 1935, *Kelly's Directory* listed only eight market gardeners. Today, though even fewer in number, farmers such as John Guerin (Brickyard Farm), John Collard (Jaicey Farm), Shirley and Malcolm White (Turners Farm), H. Bult & Son of Rydon, and Alan Bradford (Parsons Farm) continue the tradition. Alan Bradford remembers the Foster family at Steps Farm growing crops which they supplied to hotels in Bridgwater and Burnham-on-Sea. No precision drills, lifters or forward-drive tractors were available and all harvesting was done by hand.

Spudding at Impens Farm.
Left to right: Hannah Parsons, Emily Chidgey, Mary Price.

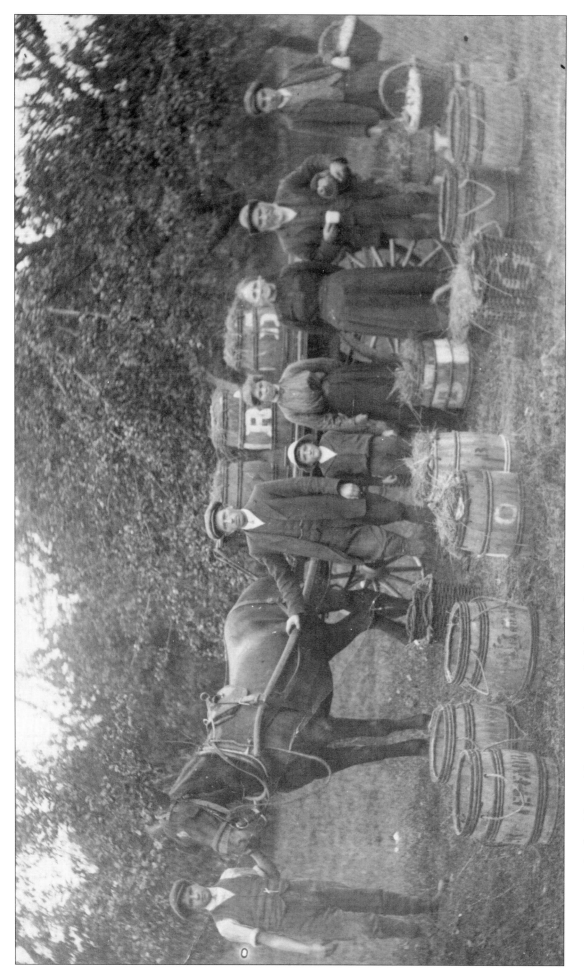

Apple pickers. Morgan apples packed in barrels with straw and newspaper ready to be sent by train to market and the coal mines. Left to right: Charles Pike, Fred Tucker, L. Whitehead (?), Mrs Sealey, Annie Whitehead, Tom Stacey, Reuben Gardner.

APPLES AND CIDER

The county of Somerset is renowned for its many and productive apple orchards, most of the bounty from which ends up being used for the delectable, thirst-quenching drink – cider. The tradition of cider-making dates back to the 13th century and by 1838 extensive orchards of apples and pears were to seen across the region. Cider was produced by the larger farmers who augmented their labourers' wages with supplies of the drink. (In the early 19th century it was common practice to hire labourers on an annual wage of £5 and in 1944 the minimum wage was £3.5s.0d. per week.).

FARMING METHODS OLD AND NEW

Farming methods have changed dramatically over the last 100 years. In the first half of the century, horses (mainly shires) provided the draught power on the farms and also pulled the carts for the bakers, butchers and other tradesmen on their rounds.

Edward Stone remembers that he helped his father with his butchery business when he was only ten years old, but from an early age, always knew that the only job he wanted was to work on a farm. At the age of 15 his father allowed him to leave school and go to work on farms in Spaxton and Enmore where he stayed for six years. He said that farm labourers in those days all had their own jobs which they specialised in. Every farm would have a 'cadler' who could do anything. He was regarded with great respect by the men, so his behaviour had to be exemplary!

Edward was known as 'the boy' who was always a single man who lived in to look after the animals at night. When he was 19 he was promoted. The live-in 'man' was allowed to have the boss' old breeches!

Another important person on the farm was the carter, a fact which was reflected in his wages (although he would also have been expected to work longer hours). Such a man was Frank Farthing who worked at Impens at the beginning of this century and whose working day started two hours before everyone else's.

Tractors started to appear in the early 20th century on the large farms, although horse power was still relied upon until after the Second World War. In 1900, after he had bought Fackrells Farm, Frank Duddridge purchased a steam-driven traction engine with a thresher and trusser. In 1906, he installed a grist mill, chaff cutter and a Petters stationary diesel engine in the outbuildings now used by Andrew Collard as a workshop. Stan and Henry Coram owned a threshing machine which they used on several farms.

Mechanisation during the second half of the 20th century increased, bringing with it greater yields but reduced employment and some of the older farmers, brought up in an era when traditional methods were used, found it difficult to change. The *Bridgwater Mercury* of 4 December 1973 reported that the oil crisis had brought several farms to a standstill as they were unable to obtain petrol for their tractors. However, this did not worry farmers such as William Foster of Whites Farm who had continued to use a horse called Prince to pull his plough. He was quoted as saying:

They're much better than tractors for the sort of ploughing I do. You can't beat the horse for ploughing something like beans. It not only saves a lot of money but does the job more accurately.

At the time William was using a plough bought by his grandfather 40 years earlier for £5!

Old Massey Ferguson tractors stored at the ruins of the old farm outbuildings at St Michaelchurch.

THE OLD AND THE NEW

Left: *Haymaking at Eames Farm.*

Below: *Frank Dunn on an early model tractor.*

Below left: *Potato digger outside Hedging Farm, 1999.*

Below: *Cutting Corn in 1929 – the boy on the horse is Maurice Finnimore.*

TODAY

Along with the reduction in farming-related employment, we have also been witness to the dramatic changes in market conditions brought about by entry into the Common Market and the changes in people's eating habits. In addition, dairy farmers have been heavily affected by the BSE crisis of the 1990s which has brought financial distress for many in dairy and beef production. Some, like the Durmans from Greenway Farm, Moon Lane, have diversified into food processing. Gill Durman has built up an enviable reputation over the years – initially with her supply of fresh duck to shops and restaurants and later with the production of her own duck pâté from the birds she had reared. She put her success down to offering 'something different' and began by concentrating on local outlets before travelling further afield to various county shows displaying her 'Taste of Somerset' goodies. Others have turned to tourism by converting outbuildings into holiday accommodation.

Farmers like Alan Bradford and the Sellick brothers still concentrate on beef, sheep (sold at Taunton and Bridgwater markets), cereal crops and potatoes. Alan says that life on the farm is not like

Jim and Gerry at work at Batts House, March 1999.

it used to be – washing sheep in the canal three weeks before dipping, supervised by the local policeman, is a thing of the past! Although farming has never been an easy option, problems today seem far less surmountable than those of years ago. With dairy, for example, herds have declined due to the introduction of milk quotas and the move to low-cholesterol foods having a knock-on effect on demand. In this area, only the Habberfield family at Bankland Farm, the Boyers and the Fosters continue to run substantial herds.

Although mechanisation has increased, some of the old crafts like hedge laying are still practised by people such as Jim Addicott, aged 86 years, and Gerry Rossiter, aged 66, from North Petherton. Jim spent all of his working life on a farm at North Petherton, starting at the age of 13. He remembers driving cattle from Durston station through the village to Bulmers Farm, North Petherton. As a youth, he recalled that one rarely got past Brook Farm without a fight breaking out between the youths of Newton and Petherton. He was persuaded to stop playing rugby at the age of 50 and still leads an active life at 86, often taking his dog for five mile walks – not bad for a man who had pneumonia and tuberculosis as a child!

Bankland Farm and (inset) *John Habberfield checking the milking equipment.*

The Church of St Peter, 1898 (with the kind permission of Somerset Archaeological and Natural History Society).

Chapter 7: Church and Chapel

There have been churches in North Newton and the surrounding area for over 900 years. In 1186 the ecclesiastical parish of North Petherton included North Petherton Church and five dependent chapelries, which included North Newton, West Newton and probably St Michaelchurch.

In 1186, William of Erleigh granted the Chapel of North Newton to Buckland Priory. This chapel probably stood on or near the site of Chapel House in Brook Street (once known as St John's Street). In the late 13th century Sir Richard de Plessis established a chantry chapel on the site of St Peters, to which he and his successors appointed chaplains until the Dissolution. In 1547 the chaplain was pensioned and chapel property seized, but the parishioners repaired the building and paid for a chaplain. In 1555 all services and sacraments except christenings and burials were provided there but by 1592 the chapel was disused, the chantry lands had been sold to Sir Thomas Wroth and with this the right to appoint the priest (advowson). In the 1630s Sir Thomas' private chaplain served the chaplaincy, which, from 1637, was regarded by the Wroths and their successors as a donative (gift). In 1742 the chaplaincy became a perpetual curacy after being endowed by Queen Anne's Bounty – a fund which supplemented the income of poorer clergy and which was provided using ecclesiastical revenues confiscated by Henry VIII and payments made by better-paid clergymen. In 1880 North Newton became a separate ecclesiastical parish including the tiny enclave of Michaelchurch which still remained a separate parish where a vicarage was established. Also around the turn of the century, Sir Thomas Dyke Acland sold the advowson to the Gibbs family of Tyntesfield, Wraxall. With the death of Anthony Gibbs in 1907 it was held by trustees until around 1960 when it was transferred to the Bishop. Boundary changes were made in 1961 and in the following year the parish was united with St Michaelchurch. North Newton has been held with Thurloxton from 1975 and with Durston from 1978.

Sir Richard de Plessis endowed the Chantry

St Michaelchurch, 1999.

with all tithes of his demesne at Newton and the tithes of the park, 35 acres of land and pasture rights (which in 1418 was worth £5). During the 17th century the annual stipend provided by Sir Thomas Wroth was £20 or £30 (and he bound his heirs to a minimum of £10). In 1742 and 1760 the chaplain received an endowment of £200 from Queen Anne's Bounty. The assistant curate, Richard Abraham, boosted the 1760 endowment by donating a similar sum. In 1827 the living was said to be less than £40 a year of which £20 was paid to the assistant curate and in 1835 the average income of the benefice was assessed as £53.

There was a chaplain's house in the village in the late 13th century which was still held by the priest in 1549, although no further reference has been found to it. The house was reputed to be at the bottom of Mill Hill, close to the church, so it may have been in the back garden of Church House, where foundations have been identified, or it could have been what is now Mill Cottage.

In 1880, £1000 was given to provide a vicarage in the village. It is said that a Colonel Gray who at that time was in residence at Great House Farm, Brook Street, gave money and land. Most of the material for the house was provided from the nearby quarry, probably the one that was opposite at the time, next to Rose Cottage. The house on the North Petherton road, now known as the Old Vicarage, was sold in 1976.

In 1418 the chaplain carried out parochial duties at Newton besides serving the Chantry and in 1425 the living was said to be a cure with resident chaplain and parishioners. In 1420 the chaplain was Thomas Chaucer who was possibly related to Geoffrey Chaucer. Some of the chaplains shared the puritanical views of their patrons, one such being Timothy Batt, the curate in 1637, who became a Presbyterian after the Restoration.

In 1815 services were held once a fortnight by the vicar of North Petherton. In 1827 there was neither a resident perpetual curate nor an assistant curate and even after the building of the Vicarage, until the 1920s, the church was normally left in the charge of the curate.

THE CHURCH OF ST PETER, NORTH NEWTON

The church of St Peter, except for the tower we see today, is only just over 100 years old, but there has been a church on the site for over 900 years. The original church was dedicated in the late 13th century. Today it consists of a chancel, nave with north vestry, a south aisle and a west tower. The tower is reputed to be of Saxon origin, having been rebuilt in 1360 and its lower parts are probably medieval, constructed in sandstone with limestone dressing. It was heightened and given new openings of Ham stone around 1635 and was substantially rebuilt and heightened in 1850 (with a Mr Dunn and a Mr Hawkins, both masons, apparently being part of the team involved in the work). There was a single bell in the tower but this was sold in 1547. In 1875 another bell and a clock were installed. The singular bell has been replaced with tubular bells which have been renovated to coincide with the millennium.

It is thought that the main body of the church dates back to 1615 but was probably partly dismantled after the vicars of Wells had used it to supply materials for an alehouse and stables. In 1635 it was rebuilt by Sir Thomas Wroth and consecrated in 1637. The south aisle was added in 1840. The nave roof, said to have been reconstructed in 1635 with older timbers, had a decorated plaster vault with an angel frieze. Displayed in the church is a picture from 1865

The renovation team who worked on the tubular bells. Left to right: Mark Goodwin, Andrew Smith and Richard Caygill.

showing the vault and the frieze (*below*). By 1879 the church had fallen into disrepair and was also too small. The then incumbent, the Revd Thomas Kerly Eaton, managed to obtain funds from the church to demolish the building and rebuild on a larger scale all but the tower. This is the building we see today – 56 square yards larger and built of local sandstone with freestone dressing.

During the reconstruction work several graves had to be removed and it is said that the remains were placed in the crypt and sealed. The Faculty papers issued in 1882 (authorising the rebuilding of the church), laid down the condition that bodies, tombstones and monuments that were moved had to be replaced as near as possible to their

original position, but show no record of who was to be moved.

The total cost of the reconstruction work was £1489, most of which was donated by members and friends of the church, and from fund-raising events. Diocesan societies gave £85, church members and friends supplied all the small windows and the Revd Eaton gave seven of the eight brass lamps. At about the same time the church room was built with the help of a £32 grant from the church authorities. The church was re-opened on 7 April 1885 and the schoolchildren were given a holiday.

In 1900 the organ was installed, replacing the harmonium at a cost of £95. Originally the pump handle was turned to the south wall and the operator was screened from the congregation. On the installation of electricity in the church during the late 1930s, the organ was turned to its present position, allowing the organist a better view of the congregation. One of the first organists was Percy Reynolds, the son of the first village schoolmaster, George Reynolds. One Sunday, having forgotten how to play the music for the organ voluntaries, Percy played an improvised version of the well-known nursery rhyme 'Pop goes the Weasel'. Some of the organists, such as Mrs Edna Coates and Graham Reading, started playing at an early age – Mrs Coates at 13 and Graham Reading, who is the present-day organist, as a young man in the late 1920s. Apart from his war service he has been the church organist for well over 60 years – surely a record!

The interior of the church contains items that date back to the early 17th century, among them the finely-carved vestry door, the screen and the pulpit, which were added by Sir Thomas Wroth. The wooden screen consists of five bays carved with female figures, all in highly detailed Jacobean dress. They portray Faith with a shield, Hope with an anchor, Charity (or Love) with a dove and the Virgin with a protective angel, depicted as the Second Eve, receiving an apple from the infant Jesus. Additional parts are incorporated in the 19th-century lectern. There are similar works at Thurloxton and Stoke St Gregory churches, although not of the same standard. It is likely, therefore, that they are copies and not made by the same carver as those in St Peters, as has been suggested. Revd Louis Henry King suggested that the screen reflects the Catholic nature of

The vestry door.

Bishop Laud, who was Bishop of Bath and Wells between 1626 and 1628 and who, in 1633, became the most influential ecclesiastical adviser of Charles I when he was appointed Archbishop of Canterbury. The vestry door that bears carvings of the Wise and Foolish virgins was originally the west entrance door. The five Foolish Virgins have their lamps hanging, while the five Wise Virgins have flames to their lamps and well-carved crowns upon their heads. The excellence of the carving is shown by the expression on the faces, the five Wise Virgins having a more sensible cast to their features than their sisters. The earliest feature in the church is the medieval consecration cross on the south wall of the south aisle.

The interior also contains a fine replica of the Alfred Jewel, given by Miss J. Lovell in memory of her parents. The 9th-century original was found in Parker's Field, near Petherton Park, in 1693 and bore the Saxon inscription 'Alfred ordered me to be made' and is now at the Ashmolean Museum, Oxford. Although more famous for his 'burning of the cakes' Alfred's great, and less talked of, contribution to our culture lay in the establishment of English, rather than Latin, as the official language (achieved, in part, by the translation of Latin religious works and by encouraging the teaching of reading and writing in the vernacular). Each copy of his treatise, which included a preface lamenting the lack of learning in England, was accompanied by a manuscript pointer from the king's regalia to help with the reading of the document. Interestingly, it is thought that the Alfred Jewel may have been the head of such a pointer.

In 1547 a gilt chalice was confiscated from the church. It was unusual, being of a medieval design (much favoured by the then Bishop Laud) rather than the traditional drinking-cup style. The plate was probably given by Sir Thomas Wroth in 1637.

The clever workmanship of church treasures is not confined to the annals of time however, for today's parishioners have turned their hands to making beautiful and useful items. In September 1984, to celebrate the church centenary, two communion kneelers were made by a team of five ladies, including Sybil Edwards (who worked the motifs), Kathleen Fawcett and Ann Tuck (who completed the gold chains and helped with the background), and Norah Chesser and Ruby (surname unknown, who also helped with the background).

SPECIAL FEATURES

Therefore it seems better to me, if it seems so to you, that we should also turn into the language which we can all understand some books, which may be most necessary for all men to know, and to bring it to pass, as we can very easily with God's help, if we have the peace, that all the youth now in England, born of free men who have the means that they can apply to it, may be devoted to learning, as long as they cannot be of use in any other employment, until such time as they can read well what is written in ENGLISH

From King Alfred the Great's preface to his Anglo-Saxon translation of Pope Gregory's 'Cura Pastoralis'. He sent a copy to every See in the kingdom together with a 'precious aestel' – probably a pointer for reading the manuscript. The Alfred Jewel featured above could be one of these aestels.

Above and left: *Replica of the Alfred Jewel on display and a drawing of the Jewel and text of Alfred's treatise by Sybil Edwards.*

Below left: *Detail from the vestry door showing the Wise Virgins on the left and the Foolish Virgins on the right.*

Above and inset: *The 17th-century wooden screen given by Sir Thomas Wroth and an example of its intricate carving.*

CHURCH GROUPS

North Newton Choir in the late 1940s. Left to right: Mervyn Franklin, John Collard, Teddy Farthing, ?, Harry Farthing, Colin Hawkins, Peter Windo, Michael Vickery, Herbert Franklin, Revd Patrick.

The wedding of Percy Pope and Mabel Marks in 1915 at St Peters Church.

Two paintings by John Buckler from the Pigott Collection (with the kind permission of the Somerset Achaeological and Natural History Society).
Top: *NE view of North Newton Chapel, 1840.*
Above: *SE view of St Michaelchurch, 1840.*

The total cost of both kneelers was £35 and the original design was by Sybil Edwards, who is also accomplished at calligraphy. A framed parchment listing the names of the St Peters vicars and drawn by her hangs in the church (*right*).

The registers date from 1778 and are complete except for marriages, which were registered at North Petherton.

The church used to have both a Sunday school and a choir, the latter being run by Albert Lock, a retired miner from the Taff Valley in South Wales. During the Christmas and New Year period the choir would tour the village and surrounding area (when necessary using the Baker Bros' transport). North Newton Sunday School started in the late 1800s (having at one time over 60 children attending) and continued until the late 1950s.

Inside the church is a manuscript giving its brief history with a list of vicars. This was given by Michael Payne, the son of Revd Sandon W. Payne, who was the vicar from 1924 until 1942. Michael wrote an article for the *Bridgwater Mercury* on 10 June 1980 to commemorate the centenary year of the parish. In it he wrote of his father:

Mr Payne also had the reputation as a sportsman. At one stage he captained the Bath and Wells Clergy Cricket XI; when he was behind a gun few snipe stood a chance, and for many years he was credited with the heaviest trout to be landed from Durleigh Reservoir.

After Revd Payne, Revd H.S. Patrick took over, 'a stirring orator in the pulpit'. Michael Payne wrote that he was known to be a resourceful man

outside the church:

to combat petrol rationing, he bought a horse; to ease the food shortage, he tried growing mushrooms in the vicarage loft, alas, his plans were not always successful!

The present incumbent, the Revd Rosemary Radcliffe, took up her duties in 1994, having been ordained in an historic ceremony in Wells Cathedral in May of that year. Prior to this appointment, she had been the first woman deacon in the Bridgwater Deanery. Rosemary has revived the Sunday School and also holds regular pram services.

WEST NEWTON

The chapel at West Newton was one of the five dependent chapels mentioned in 1186. Like the one at North Newton, it was given by William de Erleigh to Buckland Priory in that year. It was mentioned again in the 15th century, but today nothing of it remains and its location appears to have been forgotten over time. It may have been attached to West Newton Manor or was perhaps where the Dorothy Cheek School was built.

The church of St Peter, 1999.

St Michaelchurch in the 1800s captured in an early photograph and at the easel (with the kind permission of the Somerset Achaeological and Natural History Society).
Top: *St Michaelchurch photographed by Robert Gillo, c.1870.*
Above: *St Michaelchurch by W.W. Wheatley (Baikenridge Collection).*

St Michaelchurch

In the Domesday Book, the church at St Michaelchurch was called 'Michelscerca' and parts of the present building show evidence of an 11th-century church. In the 13th century, Henry de Erleigh was said to have given it to Athelney Abbey, but by 1338 it was probably under the control of Buckland Priory which paid for curates until the Dissolution. In 1541, the church acquired parochial status when a churchyard was made around it. In 1628, it was known as a 'free chapel' and during the 18th and 19th centuries it was variously described as a vicarage, a rectory, a parish church and a chapel with cure with the incumbent known as a perpetual curate. The living was united with North Newton in 1962 and in 1975 the United Benefice of North Newton with St Michaelchurch and Thurloxton was formed with Durston being added to the benefice in 1978.

In 1746, Mrs Anne Wyndham, heir to the estates of Sir Thomas Wroth, held the advowson. She was succeeded by her daughter, Elizabeth, wife of Arthur Acland. The patronage descended with Fairfield in Stogursey until 1883 and from 1897 until 1902 it was held by Antony Gibbs of Tyntesfield, Wraxal. Since 1906 the Slade family of Maunsel has held the advowson, which in 1984 held one turn in four.

In 1535 the tithes and offerings of St Michaelchurch and Buckland were together worth only 12s.5d. After the Dissolution the curate received a stipend of 106s.8d. and in 1575 was paid £6. By the mid 18th century he had acquired the tithes worth 8 shillings a year. The living was augmented between 1740 and 1790 with £800 from Queen Anne's Bounty, with which 22 acres of land was bought at Ham in Creech St Michael. Between 1829 and 1832 the average income was said to be £80 per annum and in 1839 the rent charge was £22. In 1978 there were nearly 21 acres of glebe land. No reference to a curate's house has been found.

During a vacancy in 1349, the chaplain of North Newton was allowed to celebrate at the church on three days of the week. In 1603 a layman usually read the sermon, but in 1613 it was said that there had been no sermon for three years. In the early 1600s the curate was apparently a Frenchman and from 1689 the curate also served Lyng. In 1815, an afternoon service was held on alternate Sundays but by 1827 there was a service every Sunday with Communion on great festivals. Even in 1840 when it was said there was only one resident parishioner, services were still held every Sunday, alternately mornings and afternoons, with Communion three times a year but no catechising (instruction by questioning and answering). The curates in the early 19th century were usually assistants from North Petherton and Bridgwater. William Jeffreys Allen was unusual in that when he was curate, in the early 1850s, he lived at Maunsel House although his successors usually lived at North Newton, serving both churches.

The church of St Michael comprises an undivided chancel and nave with north and south aisles, with a north tower above the porch. The proportions of the building and part of the north wall of the nave suggests that it dates from the 11th century. Some rebuilding took place in the 15th century at the west end. The east window is of the 15th or early 16th century and in 1840 the church retained square-headed windows of the same period. There were regular complaints in the 16th and 17th centuries that the lay rectors were not maintaining the church and in 1663 it was said to be ruined and to have been so for some years. The parishioners received help from the parishes of the diocese to pay for its rebuilding. A long south transept at the west end of the nave was removed after 1823 and north and south aisles of three bays were built later in the century. Both the north aisle (known as the Maunsel aisle) and the south aisle were built by Sir Alfred Slade in 1868. In 1840, there was a west gallery and an outside staircase. The communion rails, dated 1635, were said to have been removed to the priory at Chilton Polden. The church has a plain, octagonal medieval font and there is one bell in the tower dated 1670, which was recast in 1938. The church owns a small Elizabethan cup and cover and the (complete) registers date from 1695.

The church is reputed to be the seventh smallest church in England and has no electricity or heating. Arranged around the interior walls are numerous memorials to the Slade Family (*below, inset*), many of whom are interned in the graveyard. Alice Louise Earle, who was well known as a great benefactress to the surrounding area, is also buried in the graveyard.

Interior of St Michaelchurch, 1999.

NONCONFORMITY

Nonconformity was not limited to the lower orders in the parish and members of the Maunsel family, their servants and others were presented for recusancy from the 1590s to the 1620s. There was probably a meeting of Baptists at Rydon in the 1650s. By 1669 there were six nonconformist teachers with 90 hearers in the parish but by 1776 there were just three dissenters. Licences for unspecified denominations were issued in 1696, 1706 and throughout the 19th century. Licences to hold meetings in houses in North Newton were issued in 1809 and 1851. The 1851 licence was for an Independent meeting house in the village and subsequently, the home of Abraham Warner in Church Road was converted into a place of worship. In 1865 a chapel, known as the Free Chapel, was built in Church Road. In 1896 it had a Sunday school, run by the Beard family who lived in Newton House, and had become the centre of an Evangelist's district. (In 1889 an Evangelist used Northmoor Corner as part of his work area and in 1896 a mission station was recorded there.). The school thrived until the early 1920s, when the Beards moved to Huntworth. The 1891 census shows that the Evangelist was Frederick Redwood from Devon and that he and his wife were living with John Milton and his wife. Newton Chapel must have had living accommodation as the same census shows that it was occupied by James Hopkins, a farmer, with his wife, three children and servant. By the 1950s the congregation had drastically declined and the chapel was closed.

In the 1920s and up to the mid '40s, the chapel was used as a surgery/waiting room by the school dental service for two to three days every year and a subsequent owner is reputed to have found piles of teeth underneath the floorboards. From 1966 to 1984, the chapel was used as a furniture depository by M.A. Bale. Around 1984, Eric White, who ran a vehicle repair business from the adjacent property 'The Willows', purchased the chapel. Mr White converted it into a dwelling house, which in 1987 was bought by Mr and Mrs John Gouldstone.

There was also a Union chapel at Hedging which was built in 1863 and was shared with the Baptists. A schoolroom was added in 1918, around which time it had a congregation of about 40 and also ran a Sunday school. The minister was a Mr Pike, who was the station master at Washford. The chapel closed around 1964 and by 1982 was being used as a storeroom.

Hedging Chapel, 1999 and (top) *the Old Chapel, 1999.*

Chapter 8: School Days

There were several educational establishments in the parish before the village school was built in 1877. By 1835, the parish boasted 11 day schools where 240 children were taught at the expense of their parents or charities, although the majority of these were in North Petherton and are beyond the scope of this book.

As a result of an endowment from the will of Dorothy Cheeke in 1687, a charity school was set up in Rydon (opposite H. Bult & Sons) for six or more children to be instructed in English. In 1701, Henry Stodgell increased this endowment so that four more children could be taught. The teachers were paid out of the rents and profits from the land surrounding the school (some 4½ acres known as Silver Land), plus the rent from land known as Castles which was owned by Henry Stodgell. By 1786, this income had ceased but the tenants of the schoolhouse and the land contributed to the teaching of the poor for several more years. When this eventually stopped, the school reopened (in 1819) as a private establishment. An investigation by the Charity Commissioners revealed that for many years the charity had been mismanaged, with no rents being paid into it. In 1835, it changed to being run as a charity school but as a result of further charges of mismanagement it was closed down in the 1860s. It later reopened but was eventually closed in the early 1920s.

The schoolhouse and school still remain and the house has been renovated. The school buildings meanwhile resemble a farm shed and have not been rejuvenated (*overleaf*). The Cheeke and Stodgell Trust still exists to this day. In 1933, it became an educational foundation to promote the education of poor children, and makes annual awards to children in the parish to help pay for books, etc. needed for higher education.

A school at St Michaelchurch is recorded in 1770 as being run by one Mrs Slade but a century later in 1874, on becoming part of the United School Board for North Petherton and St Michaelchurch, the pupils attended North Newton School

The first headmaster, George Reynolds.

There has been a school at North Newton since 1837, the first having been set up by Sir Thomas Acland and the parents. It probably continued until being taken over by the School Board in 1875. Two years later in 1877, the school as we see it today was built and part of the old building was sold for a vicarage house. Records from 1903 show that the school then had 176 pupils. Until 1925 it also housed evening classes where, for a fee, pupils were taught such subjects as chemistry, geography, mathematics and history. Numbers have fluctuated over the years, falling to 37 in 1983 when the school was faced with closure as a result and pupils faced the prospect of having to attend school at North Petherton. However, the parents and older residents resisted this threat and today the school goes from strength to strength. As well as continuing its long tradition of providing an education for long-standing families such as the Habberfields, Fosters and Boyers (whose granddaughter, Lucy, is the fifth generation of the family to attend the school), it also attracts pupils from a wide area because of its notoriously high standard of education. In 1970, Nicholas Sellick of Lovings in Petherton Road, passed the 11-plus examination at the age of nine. He was the youngest child in Somerset to do so and went on to Exeter University at the age of 17.

The school has an active PTFA, which organises many fund-raising events, the most important being the annual 'Newt Beer Festival' which has developed from humble beginnings in 1990 into an event now attended by thousands every July. It is also the main source of school funds.

The school was built as a result of the 1870 Education Act, which brought the government into the area of education, mainly because the voluntary system could not keep pace with the growth of the population. The school was managed by an elected local board and was subject to compulsory government inspection to ensure that adequate standards and attendance were being achieved. In 1880, all children were compelled to attend up to the age of 10 and in 1883, this leaving age was raised to 11. This was extended again

Boys of the school c.1900. Left to right, back row: Willie Collard, Charlie Parsons, Jack Coate, Bill Durman, Bill Coate, Harold Greedy, Harry Acland;
4th row: Charlie Pike, Frank Parsons, Sid Higgins, Percy Pope, Jim Gardiner, Bert Stacey, Cliff Parsons, Harold Dunn;
3rd row: Edward Coles, Tom Nation, Walt Marchant, Ernie Adams, Edgar Bond, Bill Foster;
2nd row: Reg Collard, Walt Pike, ? Parsons, Percy Whitehead, Henry Franklin, Oliver Nation, George Higgins, Jack Yarde, Grenville Coate, George Durman, Frank Duddridge;
front: ?, ?, ?, Jack Franklin, Henry Habberfield, Bill Bond, Bill Trunks, Metford Duddridge, ?, ?, ?.

in 1899 to 12 (except for those employed in agriculture). From 1877, the Board paid fees for the poor, but in 1891 all fees were abolished.

The logbooks for the school survive and continue to be completed regularly to this day. They are a valuable primary historical source and should be cherished, for not only do they highlight key events in the school but they also reflect what what was happening to ordinary people in the parish. Absenteeism figures, for example, reveal many factors at play in the area; poverty was particularly rife during the early years of the school's existence and poor attendance often coincided with the distribution of poor relief at North Petherton and Tuckerton. Conditions at the school were a good mirror of those in the village at the turn of the century (when there was no running water and no tarmac roads).

The school opened on 1 October 1877 and the first headmaster was George Reynolds, a Welshman who we know, from the 1891 census, was living in the schoolhouse with his wife and five children (although the logbook reveals that they also had at least two other children who had

died at an earlier date). The initial intake of pupils numbered 77 and of these, 47 were boys and 30 were girls, each paying 3d. per week. Within three weeks of opening the intake had risen by 50 per cent to 117 with the school only being able to cope with the help of monitors to aid Mr Reynolds.

Entries for the first three to four weeks show that Mr Reynolds spent most of his time, as one might well imagine, assessing and organising the school. Reading was 'fair', writing 'not so good' and arithmetic 'very poor'.

By 12 October, there was 'some semblance of order achieved' and he was setting homework. Some parents objected to this, but he was having difficulties with 'talking' during lessons. By 22 October, the school had been divided into classes and some of the pressure was taken off Mr Reynolds with the appointment of a pupil teacher, Anna Bell, from St Michaelchurch. In the following June, William Harris joined the teaching staff.

Absenteeism was also a problem because some parents were reluctant to send their children to school. They did not want to pay the fees and they needed the children to help on the farms. There are many entries which allude to 'pea picking' being the reason for low attendance and on several occasions this was so extreme that the school was closed. Farmers were continuing to employ pupils, even some who were under age. Another not inconsiderable factor affecting attendance was the state of the roads. At this time only dirt tracks, they were transformed into quagmires by the slightest fall of rain, making the journey to school almost impossible. Absenteeism affected the finances of the school for grants were based on, amongst other things, attendance figures – the higher the average attendance, the higher the grant.

The school building initially consisted of the main body only and the annexe classrooms came at a later date. There was no glazed screen separating the classes so all of the children were taught in one large, open room. For the first six months, all water for domestic and drinking purposes had to be carried from a nearby well until one was opened in the school ground. Swings were erected in the playground early in 1878 and in February of that year, physical exercise was added to the school curriculum, while in March, the headmaster's wife taught needlework to the girls in the top class.

As there was no Village Hall at this time, the school was used for social activities, as a library, and also as a polling station, its duties for the latter lasting well into the late 20th century.

In October 1878, Reynolds opened a night school to provide additional lessons for less able pupils. However, this was restricted to boys only, because within a fortnight of opening, Mr Reynolds 'received an order from the Board that females are not to be admitted... !' The evening classes appear to have stopped after several years because, in October 1891, Mr Reynolds attempted to restart them. His log entry reads: 'Started a night school last week, but could get none to attend.' However, he obviously persevered, his next attempt being in October 1893 when he had 12 pupils. These classes, which were to last until 1925, provided instruction in a variety of subjects including chemistry.

In 1895 the school could accommodate 130 pupils but had 157 on its register. Even discounting the number of pupils attending from outside the village, the school was still oversubscribed. Subsequently, in 1896, a new room was added to the school and in 1900, the school yard was covered in asphalt, bringing an end to the problem of mud being carried inside when it rained.

In 1902, the education system was completely reorganised with responsibility for the provision of elementary, secondary and technical education being given to local education authorities. As a result of this, in 1905 the school came under the control of Somerset County Council and remains so to this day.

The following extract from the school inspectors' report at this time helps to give a flavour of life in the school:

A glazed screen is needed for the main room where four classes are at work, and where, in consequence, clearness of enunciation and audibility in reading are difficult to obtain, and undue strain is thrown upon teachers and scholars. Written exercises, elementary science and the large numbers that are taught in the higher classes are points worthy of commendation. Proper cloakroom accommodation for girls and infants are required; open sheds serve at present as cloakrooms.

As a result of this report, glazed screens and cloakrooms were erected the following year. At about this time, mains water was brought to the village, doing away with the necessity of sending children out to pump water from the well for the toilets.

On 17 April 1907, Miss K.W. Minus was appointed as Certified Assistant at the school on a salary of £35 per annum, with annual increases of £2.10s. to a maximum of £60. In April 1911, religious instruction was added to the curriculum and a period of 40 minutes each morning was devoted to the subject. At the beginning of 1915, there were four teachers at the school. On 31 August 1916, George Reynolds retired after 39 years' service, his place being taken by Frank E. Bell who joined the army the following March to be temporarily replaced by Mrs Edith Scotton. Having three heads in a year prompted this comment from the school inspector of the time:

With these three changes it is not surprising to find that the work of the school has suffered, but the present headmistress has made an excellent start, and the outlook is very promising.

The building which was used as the Dorothy Cheeke School in Rydon – now a storage shed.

Miss Lovell's infant class, 1957. Left to right, back row: Terry Thorne, Colin Foster,
Ian Duddridge, Tony Bradford, Tom Offord, Leslie Farthing, Russell Court, Nicholas Munday;
middle row: Chris Argall, Stephen Morris, Graham Bartlett, Lionel Howe, Stuart Collard, Malcolm Foster,
Valentine Durbin, Bobby Guerin;
front: Anne Jeanes, Rosemary Broughton, Angela Stone, Heather Carrot, Angela Clatworthy,
Sylvia (or Pamela?) Short, Margaret Bond.

Mrs Jenkins' junior class, 1957. Left to right, back row: Philip Irish, Harold Bult, John Guerin,
Alan Bradford, Peter Morris, Chris Irish, Charles Stone, Barry Groves, Derek Morris;
3rd row: Mary Lock, Wendy Greedy, Janet Hawkins, Kathleen Morris, Susan Bond, Hilary Carrot, Vera Boyer,
Shirley Jenkins;
2nd row: Jean Williams, Mary Offord, Wendy Parsons, Liz Jeanes, Wendy Clatworthy, Mary Bradford,
Jennifer Franklin, Sylvia (or Pamela?) Short, Shirley Ives, Margaret (?) Foster;
front: Michael Duddridge, Roger Stone, Tony Bartlett, Dennis (?) Farthing.

On 15 July 1918, Mrs Scotton resigned, and her position was taken on a temporary basis by M. Skinnard until January 1919 when Frank Bell returned to take up his duties.

In February 1921, at the age of 69, George Reynolds died and was buried in St Peters Church. He had lost three of his children – Norman, who died in the First World War, James, who the logbook shows died of typhoid in 1891 at Maesteg in South Wales, and Florence, who passed away on 9 April 1886 and who is mentioned simply as follows 'No school in afternoon, Florence M. Reynolds died at 12.40'. Both Florence and James were buried at St Peters.

In September 1923, Frank Bell left to take up another appointment and was replaced by Donald Hurd. On 19 December 1930, Eliza Boyer retired after 42 years service. She had started as a school monitoress in 1883 being paid one shilling per week and had taken up the appointment of infant class teacher in 1889, within three years of which she was on the princely salary of £30 per annum.

When Donald Hurd left for another post on 31 July 1931 he was replaced by Miss Hilda Hucker, who was soon to become Mrs Jenkins. A report in 1935 included this comment:

She has fully justified her selection, and the school is doing very well under quiet, thoughtful direction... throughout there is a pleasant spirit of industry combined with good behaviour and genuine interest in the work of the school which provides for 113 children of all ages in a somewhat out of the way and scattered area.

On 13 June 1940, 79 children and their teachers were evacuated from London to North Newton. The older children were taught in the Village Hall and the infants in the school. Facilities were shared and the necessary adjustments made to the school timetable. Air raid practices were carried out but became less frequent as time went on. In 1942, on the instructions of the school inspector, all the evacuees were transferred into the main school.

On 16 July 1948, a big day for the school, electric lighting was installed. By 1949, the number of pupils on the roll had dropped to 64, ages ranged from 5-15 years and there was a teaching staff of three. The school had another good report from the inspector but this was to be the last year for teaching such a large age range. In 1950, all senior pupils were transferred to the new Secondary school at Westonzoyland. The inspector commented that this would result in a reduction in numbers and 'free a classroom and allow extra space for indoor activities... [enabling] the head mistress to add greater variety to the excellent work she is now doing.'

Westonzoyland School received 19 pupils from North Newton in 1950 with the village school being described from then on as a junior primary school with 44 pupils on the register, ages ranging from 5-11.

On 24 March 1961, after over 30 years service, Mrs Hilda Jenkins retired and was replaced by Miss Gwen Taylor who was to be the head for the next 26 years. On July 1966, another long-serving member of the school staff, Miss Lovell, retired

Miss Taylor, the new headmistress, joins the school, 1961. Left to right, back Row: Mark Edwards, Fenton Court, Audrey Finnimore, Christine Stoodley, Brian Foster, Pamela Jenkins, Brenda Farthing, Gordon Stone, Timothy Addicot, Clarence Clatworthy, John Habberfield;
middle row: Angela Collard, Margaret Foster, Patrick Jameson, Ian Duddridge, Colin Foster, Valerie Ives, Stephen Morris, Susan Morris, Anne Jeanes, Nicholas Munday, Kay Brewer, Trudy Sellick, Tony Bradford;
seated: Wendy Bradford, Caroline Goodwin, Susan Farthing, Paul Bradford, Andrew Collard, Miss Lovell, Miss Taylor, Richard Edwards, Bryan Sellick, Maurice Nation, Simon Adams, Richard Jenkins;
in front: Jenny Pope the dog.

after 37 years at the school. The roll numbers at the beginning of September of that year were 23 girls and 16 boys.

Heating in the school was always a problem. Classrooms were heated, initially, by inadequate coal stoves. Temperature readings in January 1967 showed a temperature of 50 in the juniors' room and 48 in the infants' room. The coal heaters were converted to oil in October 1969 which appeared to be an initial improvement but by 1971 the logbook was marked with expressions of dissatisfaction, temperatures of 50-56 being recorded in the January and with the school having to close in March because of the low temperatures and the smell of oil fumes. In 1973 new heaters were installed.

The year 1970 was to see four major events take place in the school's history. Firstly, a former pupil, Trudy Sellick of Lovings, made history by becoming the first 18-year-old voter in the country (*opposite*). She recorded her vote at the school at 7am on 12 March accompanied by press reporters from all over the world. Secondly, a telephone was installed in June. Then, towards the end of the year, pressure from parents to form a Parents and Teachers Association began to come to a head. This had followed a parents' petition complaining about conditions at the school and a meeting between the teaching staff and the local Education Authority was held. The North Newton Area Parent/Teacher Association was then formed in December of that year, the subscription being two shillings per family. The fourth major event to occur in this year was that the headmistress vacated the schoolhouse on the 27 October bringing to an end almost 100 years of the head occupying the building. She completed her logbook entries at the end of this year as follows:

After a worrying and disruptive beginning to the term, the situation is greatly improved, and by the end of the term, there was hardly any unrest at all about anything!

By September 1974 pupil numbers had dropped dramatically to 31 and the first rumblings of the

Below, main picture: *Miss Lovell's last infants class. Left to right, back row: Susan Chedzoy, Nigel Salter, Ben Phippen, Victor Howe, Trevor Sellick, Desmond Duddridge, Elaine Edwards;*
middle row: Josephine Finnimore, Lorraine Duddridge, David Turner, Gregory Fuller, Robert Bowen, Michael Glide, Helen Morris;
front: Kathleen Strong, Edwin Stone, Victoria Kean, Andrew Salter, Valerie Turner.

Right: *Miss Joyce Lovell's Retirement Presentation by Edwin Stone and Margaret Foster.*

school's uncertain future start to appear in the logbook. The entry for 11 October reads: 'Education officer visited today to discuss the general school situation (numbers on the roll, etc.).' The entry for 6 November reads:

Have left school early to attend meeting for all head teachers, called by Mr Barry Taylor (Somerset Education Officer) to consider the grave financial situation relating to the school expenditure in the County.

The beginning of March 1975 saw Heather Brown take up her post as cleaner in the school. She continued the tradition of long service, retiring in February 1999 after 25 years. April 1975 saw Mrs Una Barham starting as a clerical assistant, becoming the supervisory assistant when Mrs Bond retired the following December. On 21 July 1977, Miss Taylor retired after 26 years' service at the school. She was succeeded by Mr C. Riley who stayed for just over three years. During his tenure the school celebrated its centenary on 7 October 1977 with an exhibition of the children's work and Victorian artifacts. On 12 October, a decision was taken by the managers, teachers and parents to form an official Parent Teachers Association, a constitution was agreed, and its first committee elected.

At the end of 1980 the threat of school closure once again raised its head. Mr Riley left to take up a post at Minehead and was replaced by Mr W. Allsworth, who was appointed as an acting headmaster 'pending a decision on the future of the school.' Fortunately the threat of closure was lifted early in January 1981 and on 1 February Mr Allsworth was appointed headmaster, a position he was to hold for the next five years.

At the end of 1983 another long-serving member of the school, Mrs D. Foster, left after over 30 years as the school dinner lady but she did not end her association with the school as she returned to help in the infants' class once a week.

In early 1985 the school applied to take over the schoolhouse and develop it as an additional resource. It was eventually opened

Trudy Sellick, Britain's first 18-year-old voter, outside the school.

as an annexe to the school in December 1989.

When Mr Allsworth became ill in early 1986 Mrs G. Sherwin took over as acting head. Mr David Gliddon

Mr Allsworth presents Bronze ASA Awards to Deborah Fear and Michael Bartlett.

later took over on 6 January 1987 and within 12 months was to face the greatest threat to the future of the school. As the roll had fluctuated between 33 and 42 throughout the 1980s, the Schools Review Board thought that the school should be closed and merged with the larger establishment at North Petherton. One of the reasons given by the Board was that North Petherton School was larger and therefore had more amenities to offer the children (a 'big is better' argument fashionable in educational circles). The 'consultation process' culminated in what was probably the most important day in the history of the school, 10 October 1987. A public meeting was held, at which 150 people were present. Parents and villagers turned down the Review Board's proposals and only one person voted for the merger. At their meeting on 16 February 1988, the County Council agreed to keep the school open. David Gliddon was appointed headmaster on 17 May that year.

The early 1990s saw the roll drop to as low as 24, but this was due to a new county policy in relation to the admission of reception children. From 1993 however, the roll has increased almost every year, and at the beginning of the 1998 Autumn term it stood at 68, with the likelihood of it rising further. To cope with this increase in demand a new mobile classroom was installed in August 1995 and an extra part-time teacher appointed.

All this has been achieved thanks to the professionalism and dedication of the teaching staff in the face of having to cope with the vagaries of political dogma, a new curriculum, and a (successful!) OFSTed inspection, and the tremendous support of the PTA who, through their various fund-raising activities (especially the annual Newt Beer Festival), have enabled the school to purchase a mini-bus and a new set of computers.

The school enters the 21st century having overcome the challenges to its future and is going from strength to strength. No doubt it will face further problems, but with the will and determination shown over the last 100 years these will be overcome and, hopefully, someone will be writing in the year 2100 about the school's progress.

SPORTING DAYS

Above: *Mr Geoffrey Broughton presents a prize on Sports Day, 1953.   Does anyone recognise themselves?*

Above:
Miss Lovell presents the sports cup to Felicity Kean and Marianne Mayhew, 13 July 1966.

The school triumphs on the track in July 1988.
Left to right, back row: Ruth Thompson, James Illingsworth, Kelly Morris, Rachel Pope, Lucy Bowden, Leonore Lagendijk, Michael Graham, Eva Wolfe, Andrew Bartlett, Damien Smith;
middle row: Sam Smith, Jolene Kierle, Erica Darch, Hazel Graham, Lisa Guerin, Kristan Pickersgill, Natalie Wilmott, Lloyd Williams;
front: Nigel Cossey, Joe Goulstone, Natalie Pugh, James Goodland, Adam Smith.

SPORTING DAYS

The Football Team 1997. Left to right, back Row: David Gliddon (headmaster),
Matthew Habberfield, James Cottey, David Stiles, Daniel Staunton, Carl Tinsley;
front: Edward Habberfield, Christopher Norman, Andrew Jenkins, Daniel Duddridge, Tim Norman.

Netball Team, 1997. Left to right, back row:, Samantha Gill, Lauren Burroughs, Emma Staunton;
front: Mrs Carol Becher, Jane Irish, Holly Labunski, Katrina Pegram, Emma Duddridge.

FESTIVE DAYS

The Olde Tyme Music Hall, December 1990. Left to right, at the rear: Mrs June Snelgrove,
David Gliddon (headmaster), Mrs Ann Finn;
back row (cast): Fiona Fraser, Jolene Keirle, Hazel Graham, Richard Rogers, Erica Darch,
Bryony Wolfe, Sam Smith, Christopher Meikle;
middle row: James Goodland, Nigel Cossey, Ian Shopland, Robin Hesketh, Vicky Keirle,
Nicola Horrobin, Melanie Stiles, Kirie Goodland;
front Row: Matthew Dunk, Toby Horrobin, Floria Bailhache, Mark Irish, Laura Bailhache,
Philippa Meikle, Ross Williams.

Above: Maypole dancing at Impens Farm,
Summer 1983.

Left: The School May Fair. The Queen of the
May is Lisa Guerin.

CHRISTMAS PLAYS

*December 1964, the juniors present 'Christmas Customs'. Left to right, back row: Bryan Sellick,
Mark Edwards, Audrey Finnimore, Margaret Foster, Carol Duddridge;
middle row: Angela Collard, John Habberfield, Felicity Kean, Trudy Sellick (behind), ?,
? (Father Christmas), Colin Habberfield, Andrew Collard, ?, Richard Edwards, Roger Sellick,
Richard (Jim) Clatworthy;
front: Stephen Williams, Graham Bartlett, Clarence Clatworthy.*

*Christmas Performance, 1975. Left to right, back row: Martin Boyer, Gary Ireland, Stuart Boyer,
James Barham, Fiona Durman, Mandy Stone, Lorraine Radford, Sally Moon, Nick Duddridge,
Simon Mead;
middle row: Robert Coram, Simon Duddridge, Darren Luff, Lance Duddridge, Chris Boyer,
Stephen Collard, Louise Baker, Anne Duddridge, Jane Burgess, Jane Duddridge;
front: Susan Hardy, Jennifer Durman, Caroline Salter, Norman Habberfield, Bridget Luff,
Paula Duddridge, Peter Duddridge, Jason Duddridge, Peter Howe.*

MEMORABLE EVENTS

1991 sees the school's smallest junior class on record. Left to right, back row: Matthew Caley, Christopher Meikle, Bryony Wolfe, Hazel Graham, Robin Hesketh, Nigel Cossey, Mr Gliddon (head); middle row: Vicky Keirle, Ellen Caley, Matthew Dunk, Melanie Styles, Kirie Goodland, Nikki Horrobin; front: Neil Morris, Toby Horrobin, Philippa Meikle, Jennifer Smith, Aaron Morris, Ross Williams.

The new school bus arrives driven by Penny Smith.

Above: *Mrs Violet Dunn was the first dinner lady appointed on 5 July 1948. Mrs Madeleine Cheetham was the last, finishing on 28 March 1991.*

Left: *Heather Brown's leaving 'do'. David Gliddon does the honours, watched by governors, Simon Sharratt and Ron Warren seated left, and the rest of the school, 1999.*

Discipline and Prizes

Discipline in the early days appears to have been maintained by way of a 'carrot and stick' approach. The 'carrot' was the position in class, 'the stick' being the withdrawal of privileges or corporal punishment. For example, in January 1878 a pupil was 'kept from play for a fortnight for copying in a scripture examination'. In December of the same year a pupil was 'given a sound thrashing in the presence of the First and Third Class boys' and was also put at the bottom of the class, for stealing the dinner of one of the infants.

On 13 February 1883 Mr Reynold made an entry in his logbook. It gives an insight into his philosophy for maintaining order and discipline and also shows what conditions were like in the area:

Position in class has a very great influence upon the industry and general conduct of the scholar and very great pains are taken to maintain a position once gained.

He then goes on to explain how pupils can gain and lose positions:

Places are gained for doing home lessons without error, also for general work without error. Places are lost for failures. A place is lost for lateness... Cleanliness is rewarded with promotion, but it is difficult to keep clean boots and impossible in the case of children who live in North Moor, they necessarily get over the tops of their boots in mud, even in the cleanest paths. In wet weather it is a bog.

He philosophises on the use of the cane:

I cannot make a list of offences for which a scholar is caned, as one may be caned for inattention and another simply spoken to, the latter being just as effective in the one case as the former in the other, sometimes more so. Some there are to whom a harsh word would be a severe punishment. The cane is resorted to as seldom as possible. Two or three weeks sometimes elapse without its use or its substitute in the shape of a box on the ear. But after a time, it is absolute necessary to bring it down. One penny has been spent on canes during five years.

Detention was another form of punishment, meted out mainly for talking:

For talking, and the Upper girls are the greatest offenders, a sheet of paper is divided into 8 pieces and one given for each offence to be written on, the work to be done after school hours.

Victorian Day, October 1997. Headmaster, David Gliddon, teacher, Mrs Carol Becher; children, left to right: Charlotte Foster, William Anholt, Emily Burt.

Although the use of the cane continued up to 1954, it appears to have been used only after repeated warnings. The majority of the misdemeanours were for talking and giggling in class, wasting time, unruly behaviour in the playground or poor work. However, pupils were also punished for activities outside the normal school hours, e.g. scaring sheep, rowdy behaviour in the street on Sunday, etc.

Today, discipline in the school is pursued in a manner not unlike Mr Reynold's, but without the use of corporal punishment. A set of guidelines are laid down, known as 'Golden Rules' with awards or incentives for positive behaviour (house points for effort and academic and social achievements), and disincentives for negative behaviour and the breaking of the guidelines (loss of free time, loss of privileges, etc.).

In the 1700s, one of the inducements for attendance and good behaviour was the awarding of the annual Wroth Charity Prize. The Trustees of the will of Sir Thomas Wroth had set up the charity in 1792 to oversee the use of the £500 bequeathed by him for the building of a charity school in North Petherton. The money was used to purchase land, the rent from which was used to clothe and educate up to 20 poor boys. After the charity had received a further endowment from Sir Thomas Bacon shortly afterwards, John Slade built the schoolroom (known as the Blue School) in Pound Street, North Petherton.

From 1870 the charity income was distributed as prizes for attendance amongst the Board schools in the parish including North Petherton, North Moor Green and North Newton. The criteria were extended in 1936 to cover good conduct, writing and proficiency as well as attendance. In 1980, the prize system was replaced by half the income being used for grants to schools and half to promote the education of the needy young people in the parish. There are now five schools which receive grants from the Trust: two in North Petherton, and one in Moorland, Somerset Bridge and North Newton. Each receives a grant on a

North Newton School 1998.

Left to right, back row: Carl Tinsley, Daniel Staunton, Kate Wood, Alice Sharratt, Katrina Pegram, Emma Duddridge, James Cottey, Andrew Jenkins, Matthew Habberfield, Samantha Gill, Christopher Norman, Elena Sharratt, Lucy Defriez;

4th row: Georgina Perry, Fay Sellick, Christopher Biddiscombe, Nicola Hesketh, Sarah Stone, Daniel Duddridge, Emma Perry, Gemma Hogg, Elizabeth Gooding, Nicholas Tinsley, Katy Berry, Megan Goldie, Jake Burroughs, Timothy Norman, Edward Habberfield;

3rd row: Mikala Deadman, Jayne Wood, Daryl Moore, Thomas Cottey, Hannah Carney, Holly Pringle, Sophie Carney, Dario Picken, Holly Rowe, Yavanna Deadman, Rosemary Anholt, Nicola Goldie, Rebecca Coram;

2nd row: Megan Coram, Emily Forbes-Buckingham, Elizabeth Greenslade, Chloe Parchment, Heather Brown, Ann Finn, Carol Becher, Rachel Mulcrone, Susan Hogg, Daphne Hewlett, Rosalyn Hodge, Penny Smith, Emily Burt, Charlotte Foster, Harriet Fox, Natasha Morris;

front: David Staunton, Matthew Morris, Sam Stroud-Lewis, Jack Sellick, Richard Gooding, Joshua Cook, Benjamin Sellick, Shaun Cook, Peter Jenkins, Lewis Perry, James Stone, Adam Parchment, Luke Parchment, William Anholt, Fraser Caygill.

George Reynolds and his pupils, c.1900.

A pre-1900 school group before the tarmac was laid.

'rotation' basis every four years and grants for education cover a broad spectrum from academic to vocational needs.

A condition of the will was that heirs and assigns of Sir Thomas Dyke-Acland and Arthur Acland (who owned Petherton Park in the early 1800s), should always be part of the trusteeship. Lady Gass, the Lord Lieutenant of Somerset, is the present descendant of the Acland and Wroth families and is a member of the Board of Trustees.

By the standards of the day, the prizes were initially quite substantial. In 1883, four pupils received 10 shillings each, four received 15 shillings each, another four received £15s.0d., two received £1 each and one girl was given £4.4s.0d. on leaving school, making a total of 15 pupils benefiting in one year. The entry in the logbook reads:

These prizes were regulated by age and attendance. The present rules are that to take a prize a scholar must be over 9 years of age and have made over 300 attendances. One £4.4s.0d. prize was withheld as there was no boy over 13 years and who was leaving school to take it.

Right: *A poster on the parish notice board inviting applications for grants from the Sir Thomas Wroth Charity.*

Below: *The school garden before 1962 looking towards the site now occupied by The Harvest Moon.*

Two years later only ten pupils received prizes, reflecting, no doubt, the problem of absenteeism. By 1889 the prizes were also being given to the infants and ranged in value from 2s.6d. to £1. In 1898, the total prize money awarded was £5.16s.8d. ranging from prizes of 1s.8d. to 16s.8d. Ancestors and present-day families feature among all the prize-winners throughout the years:

1898   *Alfred Bartlett, Ella Reading, Hilda Woollen*
1926   *Roy Duddridge, Hilda Norman, Daisy Clatworthy, Gordon Finnimore*
1934   *Molly Sellick, Mary Foster, Reginald Price*
1945   *Colin Duddridge*
1958   *Edwin Stone*
1962   *Clarence Clatworthy, John Habberfield, Ian Duddrige, Roger Sellick*
1967   *Trevor Sellick, Sue Chedzoy*

All worthy recipients!

Chapter 9: The War Years

The two world wars affected the small community of North Newton in different ways. The First World War inflicted great personal grief, but afterwards life went on very much as it had done before, with only gradual changes occurring in the fullness of time. In contrast, the Second World War saw less personal tragedy but greater and more rapid changes during the aftermath. The arrival of evacuees from the cities, Land Army girls, the Home Guard, prisoners of war from nearby camps and troops billeted at Maunsel House must have had an impact on the rural area which, in the main, was self reliant and had relatively little contact with the 'outside' world. At the same time, the introduction of the Welfare State bringing free education and medical services began to change lives. And, of course, everyone was also beginning to witness the great technological changes of the day.

A plaque from the school shows that a total of 124 ex-pupils took part in the two wars, but the actual number from the community as a whole would have been in excess of this figure. Walter Baker, who volunteered to serve in the Somerset Light Infantry (which took him to Ypres), and Frank Bell (the headmaster) both survived the First World War, but for at least 16 families there was much heartache. The Woollen family, for example, lost two sons, Albert and Joseph. We were fortunate to see many like Graham Reading and Geoffrey and Reginald Foster return safely from the Second World War. Also Frank Duddridge, who served in the Royal Artillery and rose to the rank of Battery Sergeant Major. A roll of honour hanging in St Peters Church keeps the memory alive of the 17 who gave their lives in the First World War and the three who died in the Second. Several were interned in the church, the headstones easily recognisable by their lack of ageing.

One member of the community who made it back was Edward Stone. He can recall his 'signing up' in January 1940 when he joined the RASC and although he only held a driving licence for a motorbike, he was allowed to drive lorries. During

John Boyer on the shoulders of Ron Dunn, a Londoner billeted at Maunsel House during the Second World War.

the first few weeks of training, he and another lad came into contact with a chap who was suspected of having meningitis. They were transferred to Bath to stay in isolation for ten days to see if they had caught the disease. During this time they were expected to either take some pills or gargle. An old soldier who was looking after them suggested that if they 'pretended' to take the pills, and subsequently became ill, they could stay where they were for the rest of the war. Edward chose to be honest and was eventually sent to Devonport, Plymouth.

There were several 'near misses' during the Second World War. In July 1940 a bomb was dropped near Bankland Farm on North Moor by a Heinkel bomber, leaving a crater 120 feet wide and 10 feet deep. Eventually this filled with water to form a large pond. It is thought that the crew of the bomber saw the glow from the firebox of a train as it passed across the moorland and used this as a target for their bombs. The explosion rudely woke Jim Foster at Whites Farm who recalls inspecting the crater the next day to see the damage it had caused. He quickly noticed a number of eels which had been blasted out of the rhynes and which were now dangling from what remained of the surrounding trees! Nearby was an unexploded magnetic mine, which was disarmed by the Naval Bomb Disposal Unit. Jim was also involved in another episode in October of the same year when he was blown into a hedge by an exploding mine in the Parker's Field area. The blast blew the roof off nearby Petherton Park and damaged the cottage at Forty Acres. Jim thought that he had come across invading German parachutists, only to find that the parachute was attached to an unexploded German land-mine. The Fosters were evacuated for a few days whilst the Bomb Disposal Unit defused the mine, some staying with relatives at Steps Farm.

On 25 October 1941, a Magister from South Wales crashed at Impens Farm, killing the crew of two. The aircraft had been seen flying low and it stalled during a turn before crashing into the ground. It was thought that the pilot had relatives in the village and was 'buzzing' them, but it all went horribly wrong. Geoffrey Broughton was the first on the scene, having ridden down from Impens across the fields on his motorbike. Despite the flames, he managed, with the aid of one of his workers, to pull one of the airmen from the wreckage, but he died later in Bridgwater hospital.

In May 1943 a lone German bomber, in an attempt to shake off fighter aircraft, dropped its load of incendiary bombs on two fields at Petherton Park, setting a hayrick on fire and causing some slight injury to sheep in one of the fields.

THE HOME GUARD

There was a fairly strong Home Guard presence in the village. The guards drilled in the Church Hall and on the school playground and the platoon commander for North Newton and Moorland was Lt. Joseph Carne-Williams. The section was formed by ex-Police Officer John Porter (Puffers Cottage, Petherton Road) who looked after their physical training and also carried out regular night patrols of the 'watch' to ensure that the guards were awake.

Geoffrey Broughton rose through the ranks to become a lieutenant and messages were taken between the various sections by his sister on her bicycle. One memory Geoffrey has is of John Porter always ensuring that the

guards he was checking on could not hear his approach. Small arms training was given by Joseph Carne-Williams of Batts House, Hodson Hill, North Petherton, and Geoffrey Broughton at Impens Farm (where rifle ranges were set up in the long garret over the stables), and at the Swan Inn in North Petherton. Training in the use of Lewis and Sten guns was carried out at the gunnery ranges at Langport – an exercise that was obviously well executed because the men of the North Newton section were awarded medals for their shooting abilities. Periodically, on Sunday mornings, mock exercises were carried out using the local Home Guard units and the regular Army. One such exercise took place near an orchard on Fackrells Farm in which a cow stall was supposed to be on fire. The village Auxiliary Fire Service soon dealt with the simulated fire but unfortunately were unaware of the cows being milked in the stall – because the roof leaked, the cowman received a soaking before he was able to stop the firemen!

Relations with the regular Army were not always friendly. Geoffrey Broughton recalls one exercise when one of the Home Guard members sustained stitches in his head after an irate soldier hit him on his helmet with his rifle butt.

Among other duties the Home Guard had to man the pill-boxes along the canal, where, because of the poor drainage, they wore wellingtons. They were also expected to check for survivors from crashed German aircraft. Several did crash in the area, one at Thurloxton where, unfortunately, one of the airmen's parachutes caught on the tail of the plane, and another near Fordgate. The Germans tended to head for the railway, and Durston signal box was used as a holding place for captured prisoners. The first time the Home Guard had to arrest a 'Fifth Columnist' (at the Clarence Hotel, North Petherton) it turned out to be a false alarm as the man had forgotten his identity papers and was a friend of the landlord!

Geoffrey Broughton's duties included the inspection of roadblocks in other areas such as Cannington and he recalls that there were frequent complaints from the Home Guard about their billeting conditions. Often they were camped near rat- and mouse-infested hayricks or in lice-infested stables.

I n the years when our Country

was in mortal danger

Michael Patrick Bryan SELLICK

who served 7.12.41 to 31.12.44

gave generously of his time and

powers to make himself ready

for her defence by force of arms

and with his life if need be.

George R.I.

THE HOME GUARD

Left: *Mike Sellick of Burnt House Farm spent three years in the Home Guard, as testified by the certificate given to him when he left.*

The Women's Role

In 1971, the *Bridgwater Mercury* mentioned that the first Women's Land Army in the area was billeted at Impens Farm in 1914. They were responding to the government call for labour on the farms, which had been depleted by the numbers required for the forces. They harvested flax which was sent to Bristol to be processed into canvass for aircraft wings, etc. and a shed was erected on an area known as Pinkley at Impens to accommodate the volunteers.

The Home Guard was not just limited to the men either, the women joined the Women's Home Guard Auxiliary section. Amongst their many activities they had to supply meals for the Home Guard at Batts House, Petherton Road (owned at the time by the Carne-Williams family and now owned by Gerald Bramley and his family).

Joyce Foster (née Bartlett) remembers the day when a mock invasion took place to test the Home Guard. The target was Churchill Farm and the invading forces, with faces blackened, approached from Moon Lane. Joyce was playing on the lawn of Churchill Farm with her friend from the cottage next door, Nesta Finnimore (née Parsons), and when asked if this was the farm, told Nesta not to tell them. They both hid behind a wall whilst the 'invasion' troops swarmed around the farm.

After the exercise everyone was invited back to Batts House for a slap up meal prepared by the Women's Home Guard Auxiliary, which included Joyce's mother, Ivy Bartlett, and Nesta's mother, Rhoda Parsons. Both of these ladies were active members of the section and both were proud to receive commendations from the War Office.

Joyce also recalls that during air raids (especially between 1940 and 1941) the family would group together, sometimes up Moon Lane, sometimes under the Dutch barn or even under the hedge opposite the back gate of the farm. Joyce and Nesta would sit on stools with their heads covered so that they could not see the flashes as the sky lit up over the area. In fact, they were probably more frightened by the 'oohs' and the 'aahs' coming from the adults and they were worried that the searchlight from West Newton would guide the enemy planes to the area.

Women were also expected to contribute in other ways to the war effort. In April 1941 women over 21 were expected to register for National Service and the women in the North Newton area were not slow in doing their bit. The days of domestic service and living-in disappeared and many worked at the nearby Royal Ordinance Factory at Puriton, being transported back and forth to the works by coach.

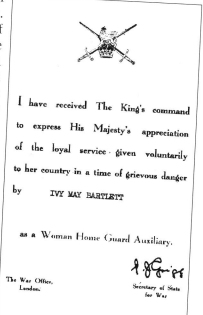

I have received The King's command to express His Majesty's appreciation of the loyal service given voluntarily to her country in a time of grievous danger by IVY MAY BARTLETT as a Woman Home Guard Auxiliary.

The War Office, London.

Secretary of State for War

Ivy Bartlett's commendation.

Other Organisations

Albert Lock, who lived at Standards in Church Road, ran the Air Raid Precaution Service (the ARP) in the village. His station was in a small room in the Village Hall and he controlled a team of 28 – 14 women and 14 men who provided a round-the-clock service (one of the wardens being Gordon Finnimore). The teams were also trained in first aid and took part in periodic exercises to practise their skills in dealing with bombs and casualties.

To aid movement in the 'black-out', white paint was painted on the walls of property in Church Road. All signposts and street names were removed and were not replaced until well after the war was over. Although, officially, all lights had to be blacked out or screened, farmers had to use unscreened lanterns and torches to attend to their animals in the fields. This may be one of the reasons why so many bombs were dropped on the moors, many of which remain sunk into the bogs at the end of the 20th century. Any identifying marks on carts were also removed.

Ruby Barrington (née Foster) can remember the drone of the German planes on their way to bomb Bristol docks and the probing beams of the searchlights in the night sky. Then the familiar voice of Gordon Finnimore would shout at the family to extinguish the lights and put the blackouts on the windows and they would take cover in the air raid shelter (the chicken shed) sleeping on mattresses on the floor.

In 1942, the vicar, Revd Stanley Patrick, formed an auxiliary fire service, teaching the members how to deal with incendiary bombs. An auxiliary police force was also formed in the area. Among its members were William Foster of Skinners Farm, Albert Collard of Myrtle Farm and Arthur Stone of West Newton.

EVACUEES

The village and surrounding area was host to evacuee children from London, the first party – of 77 children, teachers and some pregnant women – arriving from West Ham on 13 June 1940. They were initially billeted in the Village Hall until transferred to local houses.

On 17 June, schooling for the children was set up in the Village Hall. Pamela Kemp, Audrey Pearson, Jean Bennett, Pamela Jones, Bill Short and Iris and Maureen Cleveland were among the evacuees. Several children went missing on the first day and were found helping local farmers with the haymaking. Air raid precautions were laid down by Somerset County Council, drilling the children in gas mask procedures. The Council also designated the chapel as their air raid shelter. The children had frequent check ups by the health visitor whose prime occupation appears to have been to examine heads for headlice and nits.

Over the next year, the number of evacuees from the London area fell as children returned home but others from areas such as Bristol, Manchester and Epsom came into the village. In August 1942, Mr Deudney, the teacher who had come from West Ham with the evacuees, returned home. The school in the Village Hall was then closed and slowly the children were integrated into the village school itself. By December 1943 all of the school furniture in the Village Hall had been cleared away.

Some evacuees stayed on after the war. Iris and Maureen Cleveland (billeted at Fackrells Farm) married Reginald and Reuben Foster and moved away to London, to return to the parish in the 1980s.

STRANGERS IN THE CAMP!

The evacuees were not the only newcomers to the village. There were British and American soldiers at Maunsel House and Land Army girls were billeted at Old Road in North Petherton.

The influx of all these 'townies' must have been quite a culture shock for what had been a self-sufficient community but the 'strangers' were welcomed, although there was an undercurrent of restraint.

Ruby Barrington remembers with delight the children's parties given by the Americans at Maunsel House. She says: 'they were tremendously hospitable to us, entertaining us with games, sumptuous food and plenty of candy'. She also remembers seeing hundreds of Allied planes towing gliders on their way to France on D Day.

Colin Duddridge recalls pestering the GIs outside the Village Hall for chewing gum – they always seemed to have plenty of everything.

POWs

Some of the prisoners of war from the camp at Goathurst worked on farms in the village and the surrounding area and Joyce Foster still has a ring made by one of them from a farthing coin. The early prisoners were Italians and as they became trusted, some even stayed on farms such as Coxhill with the Clatworthy family, and at Tuckerton Farm with the Day family. It is said that the Italian prisoners made delicious coffee which they traded for cigarettes. German prisoners of war, however, were regarded as not so friendly and were sometimes guarded when working on the farms. However, Trevor Sellick says that his father, Mike, told him that the two Germans he had working on his farm were very reliable and took the cows to and from the fields on their own.

North Newton was also home to two employees of the Water Board who worked in Bridgwater. They were well known for speeding through the village in their car and one of them, Tim Rosebere, took part in the D Day landings. He was with other troops in a glider behind enemy lines and his task was to take a bridge, which he did successfully, helped by the acquisition of a French farmer's motorbike. He was awarded the DSO.

The Roll of Honour at St Peters Church.

Not All Doom and Gloom

Throughout the war years the villagers did well in managing to keep their morale high. There was a weekly youth club and the foundations of the future concerts were laid by people like the Revd Sandon W. Payne, Hilda Jenkins and Albert Lock, who organised what one could call 'villagers entertaining the villagers' nights. These were held on Monday nights at the Church Rooms. Musical entertainment was provided by Willoughby Clatworthy and Vandyke Warren on violins, together with several pianists. These social evenings were well supported and appeared to release the latent talent of the villagers, which is still being regularly tapped to this day in the village concerts.

Every fortnight a dance was held at the Village Hall. Music was provided by David Durman (accordion), Willoughby Clatworthy and Vandyke Warren (violins), Donald Gardiner (drums), William Trunks (tambourine) and Bill Williams, who sang and played the 'bones'. In addition, Albert Lock ran a weekly cinema.

During the aftermath of the war, some farmers, such as Geoffrey Broughton, contributed to the Save Europe Campaign by supplying potatoes and Reg Price remembers going to Taunton's marshalling yards to register details of the contributions made.

The Canal

The canal was used to transport supplies for the militia in Taunton and was considered to be an important defence, forming part of the 44-mile 'Taunton Stop Line' with its 350 pill-boxes built mainly on canals or railway embankments to form an anti-tank barrier and to accommodate men armed with nothing more than Lewis guns and rifles.

Many pill-boxes were built, and several still remain along the canal bank at North Newton. They were spaced at roughly a fifth of a mile apart and were nearly all erected within a period of about five weeks. The majority were octagonal and some built of concrete 3 feet thick.

All low-level swing bridges were also taken apart. Bricks were cunningly removed from the bridge at Coxhill and replaced with explosives so that the structure could be destroyed if required and close inspection of the brickwork shows the cleaner bricks which replaced the old ones after the war.

Ammunition for the canal defenders was initially stored in an empty cottage just over the bridge at Coxhill. (The building had previously been occupied by Walter and Rhoda Parsons and their family before they moved to Churchill House in Brook Street just before the outbreak of the war.). Unfortunately however, the cottage roof was far from watertight so the Army demolished it using explosives and built a Nissen hut in its place. The explosion caused damage to nearby property, including Eames Farm, which had to have tie bars installed to rectify the bowing of the walls caused by the explosion. After the war, Frank and Violet Dunn purchased the site and built 'The Bungalow' on it.

In about 1940, the swing bridge over the canal and the water wheel of the mill were dismantled and stripped of metal. Together with the iron discs from outside the blacksmith's forge in Brook street, the iron railings from outside Penrod (then known as Maseys), and any other pieces of metal that could be found, they were dispatched to the steel mills to aid the war effort.

A surviving pill-box located at the canal with Coxhill visible in the background.

Members of the Home Guard at Batts House.
Geoffrey Broughton is on the left, John (Jack) Porter on the right.

Batts House

Chapter 10: Life in the Twentieth Century

At the beginning of the 20th century, the principal landowners in the area were Viscount Portman, William Nation and Sir Cuthbert Slade, with some property still owned by the Acland family. Most occupations were in farming and market gardening and wagons would take the gardeners' produce to sell at the markets in Taunton and Bridgwater as well as to the local parishioners. *Kelly's Directories* from 1883 to 1935 show that the number of farmers increased from 22 to 31, whilst there was a slight decrease in the number of market gardeners from 10 to 8. Although the number of farmers increased, the introduction of machinery meant that they employed fewer workers. Familiar family names such as Bartlett, Boyer, Broughton, Bult, Clatworthy, Coate, Collard-Jenkins, Coram, Day, Duddridge, Durman, Foster, Godfrey, Habberfield, Reading and Sellick all feature at some time or other in these directories.

There were numerous amenities available which were provided by tradesmen and craftsmen and a village shop would sell virtually anything. There was a butcher, a baker and Post Office – even a fire service and a village policeman, the first being John Pope. Today, although agricultural activities still predominate in the immediate locality, the farming industry is not the principal source of employment. The majority of villagers commute to adjacent areas for work although there are a number of tradesmen/craftsmen and self-employed still in the village and the locality: John Marchant runs his electrical contracting business from Rushmead, Andrew Collard is the proprietor of A.C. Services at Fackrells Farm, John Goulstone renovates classic cars, and Andrew Smith runs his architectural business from Newton House.

In 1965, Judith Bickle, an authoress who had lived for many years at Church House Farm, published a book called *The Village of Rosemary* which was based on her life in the village. But with the closing of the Village Store and Post Office in March 1994, the village lost its last shop. Only the school and the church have withstood the ravages of the last 100 years and both have struggled at times to stay open. Breaking the trend, the Village Hall opened in 1929 and the Harvest Moon public house opened in 1962 ending 'a hundred years of drought', but even these sporadically face closure. The following is an attempt to trace what happened to some of the shops, tradesmen, etc.

Looking down Maunsel Road. The block of cottages on the left includes part of Smithy Cottage and Masey Cottage. Springfield is on the right.

The Post Office at the end of Post Office Row.

POSTAL SERVICES

Smithy Cottage provided the first sub Post Office in the village towards the late 19th century. This was also the home of the village boot-maker, Henry Whitehead. Initially it dealt only with letters but by 1894 was also issuing postal orders (although no payments). The post box was fastened to one of the exterior walls of the cottage and was cleared at 8.15am and 6.30pm.

At the turn of the century the Post Office moved across the road to the cottage at the end of a terrace known as Post Office Row (now 'Old Post Office Cottages'). It was entered via a flight of steps from the road and was run by Henry Woods who was also the village tailor.

As a result of a petition signed by residents of the village in 1903, the Post Master General agreed to the opening of a telegram facility in the Post Office, subject to the village paying £11 per annum towards the costs for a period of seven years.

Eventually, in 1906, the telegram office was opened and remained in operation until the late 1930s, by which time it had been superseded by the telephone! A public telephone was installed in the Post Office in the 1920s, but many thought it unacceptable because it was impossible to hold a private conversation. In 1962 the public telephone located near the Village Hall was installed. It would appear that no rent had been paid to the Village Hall for some years by British Telecom, a matter which has now been rectified. By the mid 1920s the Post Office was providing full postal services.

In about 1910, the running of the Post Office was taken over by Robert Stacey (son of a dairyman from the Tuckerton area) and his family. After Robert's death in a road accident at Highbridge in 1933, it was run by his widow Hannah. When she was unable to manage because of poor health, it was taken over by her daughter Irene who continued until 1972. When she retired, the Post Office was relocated to the village shop, then known as Porters.

The final closure came in 1994 together with that of the last village shop and the old Post Office reverted to a private dwelling. The terrace of cottages has been renovated and sold, the present owners being Linda Defriez, Pat and Leo Richards and, living in what used to be the old Post Office, Kathy and Keith Lowe.

Smithy Cottage when it housed the Post Office.

VILLAGE SHOPS

There were several stores in the village in the early 1900s. On the corner of Brook Street and Petherton Road would have been Porters Store which has had several names throughout its history – Sunnyside, Tuckers Stores and the Village Stores and Post Office. It was built in 1934/35 by Berrys of Bridgwater, Wholesale Grocers of Dampiet Street, on land that was part of the gardens of Nos. 2 and 3 Post Office Row and which belonged to Frank and Eliza Masey (the then village butchers). The first proprietor was Reginald Collard who, with his family, ran the store until the mid 1960s. During this time he installed two petrol pumps and also had a weekly grocery round delivering in the surrounding area. Interestingly, and as some people may remember, £1 in 1952 would have bought over four gallons of petrol!

When Ted Porter and his wife bought the store from Reginald, one of the first things Ted did was to remove the petrol pumps which, though hardly conducive to a shop selling food products, were no doubt missed by the motorists. From 1972, Ted ran both the stores and the Post Office until his retirement in 1987. He was assisted in the shop by his wife's niece, Sue Collard of Great House.

The store has had three owners since Ted's retirement. The first two stayed less than a year and in 1988 it was taken over by David and Jacqui Meikle. Despite all their efforts, they were unable to compete with the economic recession, the supermarkets and the lack of local custom and the Post Office was downgraded and its opening times reduced. David and Jacqui tried a 'use it or lose it' campaign and made attempts to gain additional support from outside the village but unfortunately this did not work and they closed in 1994.

In Church Road, on the site where The Willows now stands, was a block of four cottages, one of which was used as a small shop in the latter half of the 19th century by Thomas Godfrey. It was taken over by Percy Pope, the son of John

Steve Clatworthy gets his personality prize from Eric Morecombe and Ernie Wise in 1973.

Pope, the village policeman, in the early 1900s.

Percy moved out of the village for a while to run a similar business in Bristol Road, Bridgwater, but returned to take over the shop when it was vacated by Reginald Collard who moved to the Post Office.

Further along the road stood Stoddens House (now known as Pear Tree Cottage and part of Lynton), which was owned at the time by Percy's father. After the property was extended, Percy moved in and set up his general grocery business. On his death, his daughter, Daisy Kitts, took over the shop with her husband, Len, who also had a milk round. The couple vacated the shop in 1966 and opened a nursery business further on down the road at Portulaca which they closed in 1988 on their retirement (but Len still likes to keep his hand in).

The shop has had several owners since then, including a Mr and Mrs Herrings and Robert Pascoe who ran it as a dairy. The present owners, Colin and Chris Perry, ran it as a hairdresser's shop for some years, but it has now reverted to a private residence for the couple and their family.

The milk round was taken over by one of the great characters of the village, Steve Clatworthy (*above*), unfortunately no longer with us and greatly missed. In 1973 he was awarded the title

Clarence's ducks take a dip in a nearby pool.

'Personality Milkman of the Year' having been nominated by Mrs Barbara Walker from Maunsel Road. She said:

Among other things he gets my car started whenever it won't go... he's always cheerful, never impolite or failed to bring sunshine – he's the most likeable bloke I know.

The business was sold to Steve's brother, Clarence, who in addition to running the milk round, keeps a smallholding which involves, among other thing, the rearing of ducks who like having a dip in a nearby swimming pool (*opposite, below*).

The 1891 census shows that Mrs Elizabeth Woollen had a shop in St Michaelchurch Road (now known as Maunsel Road) and *Kelly's Directory* shows that she continued in business until at least 1914. The shop was at Maseys Cottage, now owned by Philip and Suzanne Corran.

The Habberfield brothers were grocers and bakers at the turn of the century and ran a business from the property now known as Springfield having bought it from Walter Winslade. The baking oven was a modern 'steam' oven which produced enough bread to allow the Habberfields

to make deliveries over a wide area, going as far afield as Enmore. When the Habberfields bought the mill, the shop was taken over by their sister, Emily Reading – a move taken to prevent it continuing in the hands of a competing baker. Emily ran the shop as a grocery and hardware business until it closed in the 1930s when it was taken over by the Warren brothers from North Petherton. They had been bakers there at a property now known as 'West End Stores' but they had been forced to vacate the premises by a family dispute and so moved into Springfields. They renovated the oven and carried on in business for several years until they were able to acquire premises in North Petherton again (the property now known as the 'Four Bees' located at the end of School Lane).

In the first half of the 20th century, several travelling salesmen peddled their wares around the area, including James Brownsey of North Curry who was known as 'Johnny Fortnightly' and who supplied clothing, footwear and furnishings between the 1920s and the mid '40s. Up until the mid 1930s Paul Shields Nichols came from Bridgwater selling cutlery, glassware, tableware, pots and pans and paraffin from his wagon and in the late 1920s and early '30s a comical character nicknamed 'Old Ninety' spasmodically visited selling muffins. During the same period 'Fishy Williams' made weekly visits from North Petherton.

Top: *Len Kitts' van outside the shop.*

Left: *The shop and cottage where The Willows now stands. Mr and Mrs Percy Pope and sons, John and Leonard.*

Percy Pope's Shop.

Percy's daughter, Daisy, takes over the shop.

Stoddens House, 1903. Percy Pope is sitting on the wall.

Ted Porter and Sue Collard in 1972.

BLACKSMITHS

In the early 1900s there were several blacksmiths in the parish. George Boyer had been a blacksmith in the late 19th century and lived in Rose Cottage (now The Well House, Petherton Road). His son, also called George, took over the family business, but was tragically killed in 1919 when a horse he was shoeing inflicted upon him a fatal kick to the head.

His wife, Eliza, taught at the village school for 42 years and their daughter, Blanche, remained a spinster and left the village in the mid 1950s. She kept the house which remained furnished though unoccupied and made monthly visits home by taxi in order to 'keep her links with the village'. On her death in 1990, the property was sold at auction for £44 000 to a builder, who renovated it and sold it to the present owners, John and Barbara Bartlett, in 1992.

Robert Hubbard was a blacksmith from 1867 until the early 20th century at Vicarage View, now known as Dogwoods, Petherton Road. This was his home as well as his workplace and the workshop was located conveniently at the front of the property. He is listed regularly in *Kelly's Directories*

up until 1910 as a coach and carriage builder, general wheelwright, carpenter and blacksmith, and a wagon, van, cart and lorry builder. In addition to all of this, he also undertook fire-fighting duties for the village! In 1911, he was appointed by North Petherton Parish Council to 'inspect and keep the hose and other fire-fighting appliances in good order, to see that the hose was properly oiled every year and to attend to any outbreaks of fire which may occur in this area'.

The business was taken over by Frank Culliford in 1912 when Robert Hubbard moved to the adjacent property and Frank himself gave it up eight years later in 1920, selling it to George Stone who in turn sold the business side to Ernest Osmond (married to one of the Clatworthy girls of the time) and went into farming.

There was also a blacksmith's workshop at the end of the lane, adjacent to Dogwood, which was run by a Mr Acland. *Kelly's Directories* show that James Bond was a farrier at Hedging until at least 1906 and the 1891 census shows that Henry Seymour was a blacksmith in Petherton Road and that one William Windo from Wiltshire (who set up in the trade in the early 20th century) was living with his wife in what is now known as Smithy Cottage. His forge and workshop were situated opposite, in the front of the garage of Brook Turn. Prior to its conversion in the 1950s, Brook Turn was two semi-detached cottages. No trace remains today of the forge and workshop.

Left: *William Windo, the blacksmith, and his assistant.*

BAKERS

Walter Winslade ran a bakery business from a shop in St Michaelchurch Road (Maunsel Road) at the property now known as Springfields. The 1891 census shows that he came from Burrowbridge and his wife from Fordgate. The business appears to have been successful as they had two servants, one of whom also carried out bread-cart duties in addition to being an apprentice baker. At the turn of the century the Habberfield brothers bought the business, running it as a bakery and grocery. In 1910 Edmund Habberfield bought the mill, baking there until 1924, when Philip and Walter Baker bought it 'as we had nothing much in prospect in those days'. Philip managed the mill until his death in 1935 and Walter then employed William Trunks junr to run the mill assisted by Leonard Whitehead and James Bond.

Walter was married in 1926 to Lily Marks, daughter of James and Mary Ann of Sellicks Farm, Brook Street, and he set up a baker's and confectionery shop in Sunnyside, Church Road. Walter never forgot the first batch of bread he baked: 'When they came out they were burned to a crisp and we had to mix up another lot pretty quick. But I never burned them again!' He sold seven cakes for 6d. and was known for his jam tarts. The business thrived in the village and the outlying area, and to assist himself and his wife, Walter employed Frederick Trunks, who lived nearby in a semi-detached cottage (now known as Church Orchard) together with his brother John. The Trunks brothers were roundsmen, whose cries on Good Fridays of 'hot-cross buns, all hot, come and get them' will no doubt bring back memories to old Newtonians. They also did the catering arrangements for the functions that took place in the school prior to the Village Hall being built.

The war saw the conscription of Leonard Whitehead and Frederick Trunks and when John Trunks was hospitalised with tuberculosis in the early 1940s the business could not survive. A long line of bakers in North Newton had come to an end.

In an article in the *Bridgwater Mercury and Gazette* in June 1988, Walter, who had just celebrated his 90th birthday, was described as 'alert and active as a man 30 years his junior':

Ray and Una recall the days spent with Uncle Walt with fondness. Even after he 'retired' he would get up at 4a.m. for a cup of tea. He played 'Father Christmas' for the school for many years. He took up market gardening at Sunnyside when the bakery closed, and went to market every Wednesday. At the age of 90 he could be seen at the top of the orchard, stripped to the waist, slashing at the grass with a bill-hook to keep [it] down.

Una Barham, the niece of Walter Baker, and her husband Ray now live at Sunnyside where remains of the small oven can still be seen.

Above right: *Ye Olde Bakery, Sunnyside, Church Road.* Above: *Walter Baker and his delivery van.*

CARPENTERS

The 1841 census shows that there were at least nine carpenters in the area: Robert Kearle at Hedging, Charles Tucker, George Habberfield, Thomas Butt and Charles Godfrey at North Moor Corner, and James Reading, Robert Williams, John Reading and Thomas Parsons in North Newton. The 1840 Tithe Map shows that James Reading's premises were in Brook Street, occupying one of the semi-detached cottages that was to become Brook Turn. John Reading's premises were in Church Road, probably Standards. The 1891 census is illegible in places, but does show that there were at least two carpenters in North Newton village: George Reading, who resided with his wife, five children and an apprentice at Mulberry in Brook Street, and James Bartlett, who lived with his wife and three children in St Michaelchurch Road (although it is thought that he carried out his business in the building in front of Gable End in Brook Street).

Kelly's Directory of 1894 lists George Reading and Robert Kearle from Hedging and Will Rossiter from West Newton. Many of these carpenters were also wheelwrights – Will Rossiter, for example, was the village carpenter and wheelwright for West Newton. He had nine children but he died at a fairly young age, leaving his wife to bring them up alone. One of the children, Percy, died in November 1998 at the age of 96. Until 1919, James Bartlett and George Reading are shown in *Kelly's Directories* as carpenters in the village. By this time, James would have been 61 and George 72.

In 1923, there was only one carpenter left in the village – Conrad Reading, who had taken over the running of the family business at Mulberry in Brook Street. Mulberry was converted from a barn on the site of old quarry workings in the mid 19th century by George Reading who was originally trained by the Bristol Wagon Works Company. In addition to being well-known cart and wagon builders and repairers, the Readings were also the parish undertakers. The business ceased in the late 1940s but the house remained in the Reading family until 1986 when it was sold to Peter and Alison Goldie, and a new house, Heather View, was built on the site of the workshop.

Kelly's Directory of 1935 shows that there were now two carpenters in the village, including Arthur Windo, son of William Windo the blacksmith, who set up a business in what is now the garage of Upfarm, Petherton Road, which continued until his death in the 1940s.

Mr and Mrs Masey and staff outside the shop.

BUTCHERS

Kelly's Directory shows that the only village butcher was Frank Masey, who took over the family business in 1880, 20 years after it was established in 1860 at what is now Penrod House.

The house was extended to accommodate the shop and an area for hanging carcasses. Animals were slaughtered on site in the area behind the building. After sending a joint of meat to King George V and Queen Mary, probably at the time of the Coronation, Frank was able to display the sign 'purveyor of meat to their majesties King George and Queen Mary' which no doubt boosted trade. Frank retired in the 1920s, closed the business and went into pig farming. As well as having the butcher's shop, he also owned a great deal of property in the village, including Smithy Cottage, Maseys Cottage, Dunns Cottage, Apple Tree Cottage and the Old Post Office Cottages. In the surrounding area, he also owned Hedging Farm and Wincells beyond Primmore Field. Frank died in 1937 at the age of 77. The Maseys had no offspring of their own but had brought up three children: Edna Baker, William Baker (no relation) and Cuthbert

Edna Coate (née Baker) in her pram outside Maseys.

Godfrey, and on the death of Frank's widow, Eliza, in 1943, the property passed to Edna Coate (née Baker) who rented out the house to various tenants including Walter Watts, a milk recorder, and Mr Lines (a school-teacher and the father of Molly Sellick), who re-named the house 'Penrod'.

Edna Coate recalled the days when she lived with the Maseys, in the *Bridgwater Mercury* dated 4 December 1990:

Those were the days when lamb carcasses were all wrapped in cheesecloth and sent off from nearby Durston station on the GWR. I believe we even sent meat to Buckingham Palace. The family used to buy sheep as far away as Exford and they were walked all the way back here, a journey which took four days. A lot of people were very poor then and one woman used to buy what was known as 'a head and ange' every week. This was a sheep's head and all its offal which she used to feed her family.

The property has been extensively enlarged over the years and in 1973 was sold to Roger and Ann Carrow. They then sold it to the present owners, John and Kay Robins, in August 1984.

The rear of Maseys (now Penrod) showing the workers and carcasses.

Garden Nurseries

In 1967, Len Kitts started a nursery business at Portulaca, Church Road. The business closed on Len's retirement in 1988 but he still maintains an expert interest, as can be seen by the well-groomed lawns and abundance of first-class flowers and plants in his garden.

Simon and Denise Sharratt also run another nursery in the village which can be found in Tuckerton Lane. They deal mainly with the wholesale market.

Right: Portulaca, Church Road.

Police

Up until the mid 19th century, policing was the responsibility of the Parish Council and its Justices of the Peace. Parish constables would be chosen yearly at vestry meetings for this unpaid and sometimes unpopular position. The system was cheap and probably reasonably efficient in rural areas where there was little population movement, but it did not work well in the growing urban areas where, from the early 1800s, there had been pressure to create a more efficient and professional force. The County and Boroughs Act of 1856 made police forces mandatory for boroughs and Counties and put an end to the old system. As a result, around 1880, North Newton had its own village policeman appointed with a police house provided. This appointment lasted until about 1930/31 and the building was at Stoddens House. Whilst not paying very well, the job did provide regular employment and, subsequently, a small pension.

One of the village policemen was John Pope who was stationed at North Newton for 19 years, retiring in 1915. He joined the Somerset Constabulary in 1888 at the age of 21, and was initially paid a guinea a week. Prior to being posted to the village he served at Chew Stoke, East Brent, Minehead and Durston. He took part in the police baton charge at the Bridgwater Brickyard strike of 1895 where workers had overturned wagons and magistrates read the Riot Act before the police and militia quelled the situation.

On his retirement, he bought the police house and the adjacent property, leasing the house back to the police and living in the other with his wife and family. His colleagues presented him with a walking stick and this is still in the possession of his granddaughter, Daisy Kitts. John died when he was in his late nineties having drawn more money in pension than he ever did in pay!

North Newton villagers have been diligent in their efforts to keep 'law and order' by actively

Left: John Pope in 1962 at the age of 95 years.
Right: Len Kitts with the Waley-Cohen plaque.

encouraging several Neighbourhood Watch groups to take responsibility for the safety of property. The 20th century has seen an increase in burglary and, although North Newton is tucked away in the heart of Somerset, it has not escaped the odd theft from garages, with petrol being siphoned from cars. The Harvest Moon has also been targeted on several occasions.

However, we are not short of 'home grown' heroes who are willing to have a go at the perpetrators, none more so than Len Kitts (Portulaca) who, in 1990 at the age of 67, courageously battled with a would-be burglar 42 years his junior. Len saw this man lurking in the garden of his neighbours' bungalow, called the police and, together with PC Malcolm Gillies, apprehended the thief. Len's bravery was recognised at a ceremony at Bridgwater Police Station when he was awarded a Waley-Cohen plaque and a cheque for £75.

FIRE SERVICE

Until the establishment of a fire station at Bridgwater, fire fighting was the responsibility of the Parish Council who appointed fire officers in the villages under their jurisdiction. Until his retirement, Robert Hubbard had carried out the necessary duties. When Frank Culliford took over Robert's business he also inherited the fire officers' duties. To assist him in dealing with fires, he had a team of four men who were each paid half-a-crown for the first hour and one shilling for every hour afterwards. The captain of the fire crew, Frank Culliford, was paid one guinea. All the fire crew had identification caps and the fire-fighting appliances were carried to the fire scene in a builder's handcart.

On 2 January 1920, Frank's retainer was raised to £2 per annum and when he gave up the business and moved to Hedging in 1921, his place was taken by Ernest Osman. He is shown in *Kelly's Directory* to be a coach and motor body builder, agricultural machinist, repairer, wheelwright and blacksmith and had previously worked for Conrad Reading before setting up his own business.

One of the fires the service dealt with occurred at one of the tied cottages of Impens Farm in 1922. On Osman's resignation in 1926, Arthur Windo, the blacksmith, was appointed, and the pay for the fire team members was raised to five shillings for the first hour and half-a-crown for every hour afterwards. Arthur was to be the last to hold this position as Bridgwater Fire Station was opened soon after his appointment. It is interesting to note, however, that even today, Somerset Fire Authority rely heavily on retained fire personnel who are part timers, many of them from outlying villages.

SERVICES

Electricity came to the village in the late 1930s but only initially to the church, the school and a limited number of wealthier homes. After 1945, all homes were on mains supply. Street lighting was installed in the mid 1950s.

Before the arrival of mains water, the village was supplied from numerous wells with the water having to be drawn manually by pump or bucket and windlass. Mains water came to the village in 1905, but was not connected in outlying areas such as Hedging, West Newton and Rydon until some time in the 1920s. However, this did not mean that all houses would have had running water and flush toilets. Initially, only people who could afford the connection charges and free-standing properties were supplied with running water and terraced houses had to be content with a standpipe or hydrant. Some houses still had primitive toilet arrangements up until the late 1940s. The sewage system which had been installed at the same time as the mains water was unable to cope with the existing houses and the new properties which had been built after the war, so in 1964/65 a new, up-dated system was installed. Prior to the laying of road surfaces in 1905, roads were compacted earth (*below*), which turned into quagmires in the rain.

Ceremonial arch erected for the Coronation of Edward VII across Petherton Road between Upfarm (left) and Dogwoods (right), 9 August 1902. This was in the days before the roads in North Newton were surfaced.

A day Out in the 1930s. 1. Arthur Windo 2. Len Pope 3. Bert Hurford 4. Metford Duddridge 5. May Hurford 6. George Habberfield 7. Melville Lock 8. Ada Windo 9. Linda Clatworthy 10. ? 11. Jack Trunks 12. Moira Lock 13. ? 14. Rose Higgins 15. ?. 16. Alan Higgins 17. Dave Durman 18. ? 19. Desmond Lock 20. ? 21. Lily Higgins 22. Edith Snook 23. Walter Parsons 24. ? 25. Cynthia Higgins 26. ? 27. ? 28. ? 29. ? 30. ? 31. Rhoda Parsons 32. Eva Yarde 33. ? 34. Dorathy Chedzoy 35. Emily Chedzoy 37. Albert lock 38 and 39. Guy and Leslie Fursland (drivers).

Chapter 11: Village Pastimes

Different activities have been taken up and dropped over the years and North Newton has probably suffered socially with the passing of the decades, just as other small communities have. However, there is never a need for an excuse to have a 'get-together' and the villagers have always taken every opportunity to enjoy themselves. Whether for a special occasion or just to get away and have a good time, there are inevitably plenty of takers!

People have moved in and out, come and gone, and various groups have been formed – some of them enjoying great longevity and others lasting but a while.

North Newton residents on a trip to Cheddar in 1922.

THE WOMEN'S INSTITUTE

The first meeting of the North Newton branch was held in the village on 3 April 1964 with over 70 members, now down to a handful. In 1965 all the members contributed to a fine scrapbook called 'Village Life in North Newton 1965' which gave a wonderful insight into how things were and celebrated the 50 years of the Women's Institute from 1915. The activities enjoyed at the meetings

have not changed over the years but new areas of interest crop up from time to time and members always make guest speakers welcome. Pat Richards (2 Old Post Office Cottages) has supplied a list of notable guests: Clive Gunnel of TV fame gave an insight into showbusiness; unusual subjects have been presented by a 'Beefeater' from the Tower of London; and the members have been entertained and serenaded by Ray Budd of the original 'Black and White Minstrel Show'.

Sarah Evans (Tuckerton Farm) shared her Nepalese experience with everyone and Ginny Sharratt talked about her four-year stay in Hong Kong. Many speakers have transported the members around the world with talks and slides.

The WI has also had visits from a prison officer, a Salvation Army Major, and Dennis Gill, a representative of Guide Dogs for the Blind, spoke of their work in the community. Talks have also included subjects such as gardening and the countryside, with Exmoor and Somerset being among the most popular topics. And there is no shortage of volunteers when reflexology, aromatherapy and massage are on the agenda!

The group thoroughly enjoy their trips which are many and varied, including more than one to Harveys of Bristol (hic!), nights at the theatre, rambles, craft workshops, picnics, and visits to other branches. The members always show great talent in areas of arts and crafts, and regular competitions are held when they come into their own.

These are not the only things that the members are good at! Representatives periodically attend scrabble competitions at county level, notably Margaret Shepherd and Sybil Edwards.

Left: *Sampler made by the WI ladies.*

Above: *The WI
Committee 1999. Left to
right, back row: Sybil
Edwards, Pat Richards,
Penny Berry, Elizabeth
Habberfield;
seated: Sylvia Rutter,
Althea Reading
(President), Ginny
Sharratt.*

Left: *Vera Lock (née
Reading) dressed for the
treat of representing the
North Newton WI at
Buckingham Palace.*

VILLAGE HALL

The Hall forms one of the main focal points in the village and helps to bring everyone together as much as possible, perpetuating a stronger sense of community.

A committee was set up in 1920 to initiate the building of a village hall to serve the parish and to look for a suitable site. This did not present itself until 1929 when the property known as Standards mysteriously burnt down. It was a cob-built, thatched house (the name of which has now been passed on to the property next to the Hall). In the late 19th century, the house was occupied by Francis Duddridge, his wife, Sarah Ann, and their three daughters, Alice, Daisy and Mary. The Duddridges vacated the farm at the turn of the century to move to Fackrells Farm on Petherton Road and the building was then taken over by Walter Gardner and bride Alice (née Adams). The couple stayed at Standards for about 27 years, bringing up two sons there, Reginald and Donald. In 1928 they moved out to live with Alice's widowed mother, Charlotte Adams, at Chapel Hill Farm in Brook Street and it was shortly after this that the farm burnt down.

Prior to the Village Hall being built, nearly all social events took place, inconveniently, in the school. The committee, which had amongst its members ex-Police Constable John Pope, Mr and Mrs Albert Broughton, Mr and Mrs Masey, Mr and Mrs Francis Duddridge and Walter and Philip Baker, was charged with raising funds to build a village hall. With financial and legal aid from the then tenant managers at Maunsel Grange, the committee was able to purchase the site. Stacey Brothers of Westonzoyland constructed the building to a design based on Pawlett Village Hall and it was opened in November 1929 by Mrs Alice Louise Earle, tenant manageress at the Maunsel Estate (together with Mrs Jemmett Brown). Reg Price recalls the opening ceremony:

There was an amusing incident concerning the opening ceremony. Ex-policeman, John Pope, who was the secretary of the fund-raising committee, had asked Mr Foxwell, the head gardener at Maunsel, to get a presentation bouquet of flowers. Unfortunately he did not say which occasion it would be for and Mr Foxwell didn't guess either! So he gathered the flowers from Maunsel gardens and after Mrs Earl was presented with her bouquet she was heard to whisper to those around her that she knew where they had come from, but she accepted them in the spirit in which they were given!

If the Hall hadn't been officially opened in 1929, there might well not have been a Golden Wedding celebration in 1985 for Tom and Gladys Vickery who met at the opening. Gladys was born at Coombe St Nicholas, moving to North Newton with her parents where her father had a

One of the Christmas dances in the 1940s. Does anyone recognise themselves?

See How They Run, a play by the Drama Club. *Left to right: Graham Hawkins, Edward Stone (seated), John Collard, John Hook, Len Kitts, Laura Bond, Joan Sellick, Colin Hawkins, Susan Bond.*

An early fancy-dress dance.
Those present include: front: 'Wet and Dry' (Mr and Mrs Thomas from Puffers Cottage), Reg Brewer,
Olive Adams, Percy Pope (in top hat), Sheila Hale;
behind (to the left of the picture): Fred (Shepherd) Adams and Reg Collard-Jenkins;
back (left to right): ?, Len Pope (above umbrella), Lily Foster, Heather Randall, Pat Williams, Mervyn Haggett;
to the right: Leslie Watts, Mrs Porter.

smallholding. She eventually worked as a parlour-maid at Maunsel Grange. Tom came from North Petherton where he had worked for a local builder and farmer for 10 shillings a week. They married at St Peters Church on 25 October 1935 and lived in Maunsel Lodge. Tom said at the celebrations 'I have a contented mind and a marvellous wife'.

Weekly dances were held and amongst the dance bands that played up until the late 1950s were: The Denza Dance Band (Vera Reading on the piano, Willoughby Clatworthy on the violin and 'Obby' Strong beating it out on the drums); The Clubmen; Colin Day and his Quantock Vale Orchestra; The Willoughby Clatworthy Trio; The Victory Dance Band (led by a Mrs Burt from Stogursey and consisting of three piano accordions, piano and drums); and Mrs Jackson's Premier Band. Gerald Bramley of Batts House (Newton Road, North Petherton) played in both the Victory Dance Band and Mrs Jackson's Premier Band. During the war, as well as being used as a school for the evacuees, the Village Hall also housed a weekly cinema which was run by Mr Lock.

Having to compete with television, cinemas, nightclubs, etc., the Village Hall is not the 'social centre' of the village in quite the same way that it used to be, but a few dedicated people do their utmost to keep it economically viable – a task made all the more challenging by the seemingly constant introduction of new legislation which calls for expensive upgrades to amenities.

In 1965 there were 24 members on the committee, whereas at the end of the 20th century it is just under half that figure. The first Secretary was John Pope and two of the most notable members

The Village Hall, 1999.

are Dennis Collard-Jenkins, who gave many many years of dedicated service, and Gordon Finnimore of Starkeys Cottage. Gordon was invited on to the committee when he turned 18 in 1933. He became a secretary in 1946, and continued in this role until 1985. By this time he had also taken on the responsibility of being a treasurer which he served as from 1965 until his retirement in 1995 – a total of 49 years! The Sellick family of Burnt House Farm needs particular mention too. Mike Sellick served as a committee member, and later as a trustee, until his death in 1996. His wife Molly served as a committee member and was made Chairperson and later President (the only person to be given this title) when she retired through ill health. The link with the Hall continues today as Bryan (Molly and Mike's eldest son) is a trustee, and their youngest son, Trevor, is a committee member. Diane Coram of Hedging Farm is the present Chairperson, Susan Hughes of North Petherton is Treasurer, and Kay Robins of Penrod House is Secretary.

In 1965, approximately £110 per annum was sufficient to cover the running expenses of the

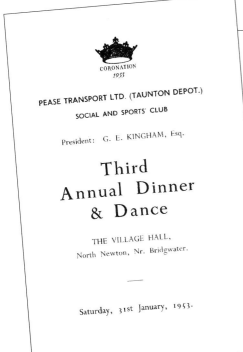

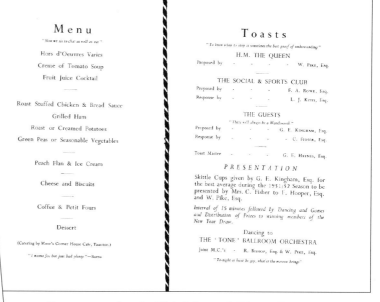

Programme for the Third Annual Dinner Dance, 1953.

building and the hire charge was £34. Today the annual running expenses are £1500 and the cost of hiring the Hall is £50 per day or £30 for the evening.

Today the Village Hall is used for, amongst other things, occasional dances and regular whist drives, and the school uses it weekly for gym class. When required it is used as a polling station, monthly WI meetings and wedding receptions. It is also the venue for the North Newton concerts, which are held regularly.

Major repairs to the building become more of a problem as time goes on, but as the property was built such a long time ago it is not surprising! The roof was replaced in 1992 at a cost of £9000 and in 1998 the windows were replaced at a cost of £7000. All this expenditure takes a lot of fund-raising and pleading to local councils for grants and the committee is constantly trying to come up with new ideas as well as re-circulating those which prove to be the most popular, i.e. weekly draw tickets, dances, fun days (organised with the cricket team), demonstrations and quiz nights. The concert group also donate their proceeds to the funds. The next project being considered is to replace the floor and up-date the central heating.

As the Village Hall is the main focal gathering point, the committee joins in other organisations' events whenever possible and whenever invited. Subsequently, other organisations and groups use the Hall in return. One joint venture that was a particular success was the VE Day Celebrations involving all of the groups in the village. A committee was formed with representatives from each group and events were held for the whole weekend of 8 May 1995. The final event was a dance held in the Hall, which was nearly bursting at the seams! A great time was had by all.

Above: *The Annual Church Produce and Flower Show 1988. Left to right, back row: Molly Sellick (John Lang Trophy), Ann Tuck (Pam Cridland Trophy), Margery Jenkins (Steps Farm Trophy); front: Fiona Fraser (Molly Sellick Trophy), Violet Dunn, Ray Barham (W. Cridland Cup and George Barham Memorial Trophy).*

Right: *The presentation of the cheque from Nuclear Electric towards the cost of the new roof. Left to Right: Kay Robins (Secretary), Keith Horton (Nuclear Electric), Geoff Holt (roofing contractor), Gordon Finnimore (Treasurer), Ann Holt (Chairperson).*

THE VILLAGE HALL CONCERTS

The 'villagers entertaining the villagers' has been a tradition since the opening of the Hall. No information is held of the details of those involved in the organisation of these concerts in the early days although a photograph does survive (*below*). The Village Hall has been the venue for regular concerts since 1978 and they have taken place almost every year since then, with the local talent shining through at each performance!

The idea to raise funds through these concerts came from Mary Collard (Fackrells Farm) who rounded up a group of fellow enthusiasts who were prepared to show off what they could do and put on their first performance in October 1978, the proceeds of £150 going to church funds. Mary organised the whole event, taking responsibility for the arrangements, selling the tickets and generally encouraging everyone. She also kept an account of the ten years of her involvement up to 1988.

The concerts always include an element of comedy and the villagers look forward to the next show to see who will be 'taken off' this time. The group is never short of raw material taken from events and characters from the village itself.

From 1988 onwards, new people joined the group and the concerts took on a new look, providing opportunities for other talents to be demonstrated. In the early days 'live' music was provided by Jack Chesser and his trio – today, it is mostly provided by sophisticated electrical equipment. Costumes are frequently made by the ladies of the group, but the expertise of Beverly Farr can usually be relied upon to add a touch of professionalism to the outfits. Unlike London's West End, the shows in North Newton do not have the luxury of hundreds of back-stage supporters, but those who do help work jolly hard. Unfortunately, the performers are also expected to turn their hands to other jobs – writing the scripts, preparing dance routines, erecting the portable stage, getting the electrics and lighting sorted, selling the tickets, and cleaning up afterwards. Local organisations have benefited from the proceeds over the years, but the group later decided that all profit was to be donated to the Village Hall.

A mention of the village concerts cannot go by without specific reference to one person in particular – the late Steven Clatwothy of Coxhill Farm. Steve was loved by everyone and could always be relied upon to give the best performance every time he went on stage. He could change into any character required in the sketches, often also having written the sketch himself. He could 'ad lib', putting off his fellow players with his great sense of fun and was a fantastic stand-up comedian who could keep the audience in stitches whilst the scenery was being changed behind the curtains. Steve appeared in every concert held, together with other members of the Clatwothy family who never fail to entertain the audiences in their own inimitable style!

An early concert during the 1930s. Left to right, back row: Kathleen Whitehead, Ena Collard, Emmie Woollen, Winnie Foster, Phyllis Hope; front: Nellie Meade, Olive Porter, Doris Finnimore.

VILLAGE CONCERTS

Above: *The Black and White Minstrels, late 1970s. Left to right: Pat Richards, Mary Collard, Sylvia Hillman – does anyone recognise the others?*

Left: *Steve Clatworthy performing in 1981.*

Below: *John (Jack) Chesser, late 1970s.*

VILLAGE CONCERTS

Above: *Steve with Martin Perry in the 1980s.*

Right: *The Spice Girls, 1997, with Roger Grimshaw as 'Ginger Spice', Tony Hughes as 'Posh Spice'.*

Below: *Violet Dunn, still performing in her 80s.*

The first cricket team in 1946. Left to right, back row: Clare Mayled, Cuthbert Godfrey, Fred Adams, Major Randall, Harry Johnson, Gordon Finnimore, Eric Knoght, Mervyn Ingram, Bill Whitehead, Ivor Ingram; front: Revd Patrick, Mike Sellick, Stuart Norman, Jack Sellick, Len Kitts, Albert Giles, Alan Sellick, Jack Porter.

THE CRICKET CLUB

The Cricket Club was formed in 1947 after the Second World War. Edward Stone recalls:

I was one of the founder members because I was the only one who had a motor mower. Revd Patrick approached me to use the mower until Jack Porter retired and took over. My involvement with the club was short-lived though. We were practising one day and I was on the receiving end of Alan Sellick's fast bowling! He bowled to me extremely fast and the ball hit me in the face. They thought that my jaw was broken so sent me off to see Mr Winkworth, a specialist in Taunton. He took one look at the X-ray and confirmed it. I was hospitalised for a month. I had to pay £50 for my care as the club wasn't insured. Poor Alan offered to look after my cow whilst I was away.

Initially the team played on a field at Impens Farm until 1960. The first official groundsman was ex-policeman Jack Porter of Puffers Cottage. From Impens the club moved to a field on Spanish Hill owned by John Collard where they remained until 1968. From 1969 to 1976 the club re-located to the Civil Service Club in Taunton.

In the meantime, the Playing Field Association (formed in the village in 1973) acquired the playing field in Tuckerton Lane. The pavilion was built over a period of four years between 1973 and 1977 (well Rome wasn't built in a day, was it?) and the adjoining car park prepared in 1976, so when the wicket was ready the following year the cricket club returned to the village. In the early days, the team was only involved in friendly matches against other village teams.

The team joined the Bridgwater Cricket League at Division Five in 1979, playing on Saturdays. They were promoted to Division Four in 1988 rising to the highest position of 5th place a year later in 1989. Unfortunately, they were relegated to Division Five again in 1991 where they remain in 1999. The Sunday team concentrates on playing 'friendly' matches. Worthy of note is the fact that Colin Duddridge is the longest-serving member of the Cricket Club having joined at the age of 13 in 1948.

The Cricket Team in the early 1980s. Left to right, back row: Norman Stone, Harry Liddle, Terry Hembrow, Ron Gardner, Keith Paskin, Colin Palmer, Bryan Sellick, Alan Coram, Colin Duddridge; front: Paul Bishop, Eddy Stone, Alan Bradford, Graham Bishop, Mark Carrow, Gordon Stone.

The Saturday Cricket Team in 1999. Left to right, back row: Trevor Gibbs, Simon Gardner, Ian Bishop, Nick Owen, Paul Lambert, Pete Brownsey, Steve White;
front: Eddy Stone, Chris Barrington, Bob Abrams, Bryan Sellick.

The Sunday Cricket Team in 1999. Left to right, back row: David White, Pete Welham, David Welham, Ian Bishop, Max Hooley, Paul Lilley, Steve White, Chris White;
front: Bob Abrams, Alan Bradford, Colin Duddridge, Nick Owen.
Missing from the photos: Mark Barham, Ron Gardner, Ruddy Plummer, Chris Busby.

North Newton Rams who, despite only running for a very short time during the late 1970s, did beat North Petherton Firsts! Left to right, back row: Richard Edwards, Colin Riley, Dick Fear, Clarence Clatworthy, Mark Edwards, Dave Darch, Jim Clatworthy, Andrew Collard;
front: Mike Coles, Tony Bartlett, Steve Clatworthy, Gordon Stone, Bryan Sellick, Roger Sellick, Trevor Sellick.

FOOTBALL CLUB

Several attempts have been made, at one time or another, to form a football team and information of their early days has proved elusive except for a rare photograph which shows a large membership at the Annual Dinner in the Village Hall just after the Second World War *(below)*.

Alan Bradford was one of the villagers to form a team in the late 1970s from those who played for Bridgwater Young Farmers. These included Richard Jenkins, John and Colin Habberfield, and Alan and Tony Bradford. They were called North Newton Rangers and joined the Bridgwater and District Sunday League with a strong team. They were the runners-up for the Harvey Cup in 1988, and moved from Division Three to Division Two before enthusiasm waned and the team folded a few years later.

In the late 1990s a new team began for the small boys of primary-school age. They meet on Saturday mornings at North Petherton, playing matches against other local lads and will hopefully pave the way for a permanent village club.

North Newton Rangers in the late 1970s.
Left to right, back row: Bob Abrahams (Manager), Colin Habberfield, John Carey, Keith (Ivor) Ingram,
Guy Richards, John Habberfield, Alan Bradford (Captain), Keith Paskin;
front: Keith Taylor, Andrew Baker, Richard Jenkins, Tony Bradford, Nigel French, Gavin Ireland, Mark Carrow.

North Newton Rangers in the 1980s.
Left to right, back row: Martin Acland, Tony Bradford, Paul Donaghue, Keith Ingram, Howard Groves,
Andrew Derham, Sean Ives, Alan Bradford (Manager);
front: Gavin Ireland, Paul Bishop, Mark Carrow, Eddy Stone, Paul Duddridge, Trevor Gibbs, Ringo (mascot).

LADIES ROUNDERS TEAM

Believe it or not, North Newton has a thriving Ladies Rounders Team totally dedicated to winning the 'friendly' Bridgwater League! The team was the brainchild of Rita Pope who lived at Churchill Farm. Rita is a keen netball player and with a few fellow enthusiasts decided, back in 1984, that it would be a good idea to hold a few matches during the summer. She gathered together some local ladies, many of whom had not played rounders since their school days. A good time was had by all and since then the team has not looked back!

The friendly league was formed a few years later as more and more teams joined in from Bridgwater town and the surrounding villages. Currently there are 15 teams in the league. North Newton has always been in the top three teams and has won the cup many times, with write-ups in the *Bridgwater Mercury*.

North Newton Ladies Rounders Team 1999.
Left to right: Daphne Turner, Dawn Fothergill,
Amanda Hicks, Chris Shaw, Dora Hinkley,
Chris Chard, Clare Trask, Hannah Read,
Alison Read, Rita Pope (Captain), Kay Robins.
Absent are Rachel Pope and Maggs Higgs.

YOUTH CLUB

Several efforts have been made over the years to run a youth club but, alas, none has lasted. The first club started in the 1930s when Revd Payne presided at the church, and meetings were held in the Church Rooms. The leader was Albert Charles Locke, who was also Head Warden during the Second World War in charge of the air raid activities. The club continued during the war and Albert often recruited his 'wardens' from among its members – members who often had no prior notion that they would be doing wardens' duties!

Ray Barham (Sunnyside) and a county youth leader, Roy Stanford, formed a youth group in the mid 1970s, members of which also met in the Church Rooms. Activities included table tennis, pool, snooker and bagatelle and refreshments. Eventually the group moved to the Village Hall when Ray's wife, Una, joined in to help together with Mary Foster. They had about 30 members initially but these dwindled down to one and the club was wound up in the mid 1980s.

In 1988, Barry and Sandy Finch, together with Les Pickersgill, formed the latest club which stayed open until 1997. Sandy qualified as a Somerset Youth Worker and became the club's leader, supported by Barry as Chairman.

The club was run in the Village Hall giving the youth of the village the opportunity to meet to play indoor sports and enjoy various activities and a tuck shop. Visits were also arranged to outside venues, notably a visit to London's 'Cardboard City' in March 1994 where the youngsters were given a stark insight into the contrasts between their own lives and the reality of living on the streets.

OVER FIFTIES CLUB

This was previously called the Over Sixties Club, but because of the drop in membership in recent years the age for members was lowered to encourage new recruits. Mrs Cook, mother of Revd Cook, formed the club and when she left the parish in December 1982, the members presented her with a silver salver. Mrs Violet Dunn was the main organiser for almost 21 years but stood aside for 'someone younger' to take over in December 1983 when she was 82 years of age! Mrs Avis Williams took her place.

Main activities involved the crafting of wooden and knitted items which were sold to create funds to keep the club going. When Zena Bradford died, she bequeathed a sum of money to the club which was used to cover costs. The members had been meeting once a fortnight in to play bingo and have a chat and tried to have two meals out a year, either at The Harvest Moon or The Swan Hotel in North Petherton. Sadly, in June 1999, the decision was made to disband and the remaining funds held at the time were kindly donated to the Village Hall and St Peters Church.

North Newton Moonrakers. Champions of the Bridgwater Town and District League Division Three.
Left to right, back row: Ron Brooks, Ron Gardner, John Durman, David Baker, Robert Pascoe, Ian Duddridge;
front: Roly Law, Steve Clatworthy, Mike Bowden (landlord), John Collard.

THE SKITTLES TEAMS

Gordon Finnimore (Starkeys Cottage) can remember skittling in a loft at Impens Farm when he was a young man. It was owned by Geoffrey Broughton and the floor was so flat that proper skittling boards were not needed. Later, the interest in skittles moved to the Village Hall after it was built in 1929. Originally, the game was played in the skittle alley located behind the main building and this continued until after the Second World War (although occasionally skittles would be played outside when special boards had to be laid down). The people who played on a regular basis were the 'movers and shakers' of their time, like the Maseys, Collards, Godfreys and Fosters.

These people were usually behind most of the activities that went on at the time – with the Hall, the church and the school – and were often active committee members and school governors. Edward Finnimore and Reg Price were 'stickers-up' in their youth for five or six years. It was the men who played mostly, but on social occasions such as fêtes, celebrations, etc. the women would also join in. One of the attractions was a competition called 'skittling for a pig' in which the popular prize of a suckling pig supplied by a local farmer was on offer.

The 'shed', as the old skittle alley has now become known, is still in use as a storage area for the Village Hall equipment. The modern teams of skittlers in the village have been based at The Harvest Moon since 1962, after having to use public houses in North Petherton when the game became more serious with the advent of league matches.

Stuart Scriven remembers when his family was at The Moon and his father ran competitions, donating a lamb or a calf as the main prize. His mother was well known for her wonderful skittle suppers! Separate teams of men and women compete in the Bridgwater League. As well as the 'senior' members' team, 'The Moonrakers', Alan Bradford formed a second men's team in the late 1970s with a nucleus of cricketers. They had to start in Division Six but have worked their way up to Division One and have walked away with the Taunton Cider Cup on two occasions.

An Early Photo of the skittlers, c.1930. 1. Henry Coram 2. Grenville Coate 3. Cuthbert Godfrey 4. ?, 5. Alice Collard 6. ? 7. Elisa Masey 8. Frank Masey 9. Edna Baker 10. ? 11. ? 12. Bill Foster 13. ? 14. Sarah Duddridge 15. Cyril Cousins 16. Albert Collard 17. Nellie Godfrey 18. ? 19. Lily Foster 20. Walter Pike 21. Violet Dunn 22. Florence Whitehead.

Winners of the Taunton Cider Cup, 1983.
Left to right, back row: Richard Edwards, Trevor Sellick, Bryan Sellick, Eddy Stone, Tony Bradford, Gordon Stone;
front: John Guerin, Colin Duddridge, Howard Groves, Alan Bradford, Sean Ives (sticker-up).

North Newton Ladies 'A' Team, 1999.
Left to Right: Denise Gilbertson, Sharon Brook, Jean Brooks, Donna Bartlett, Judy Grimshaw,
Mabs Habberfield, Amanda Heayns, Diane Coram; absent: Debbie Carrow.

CARNIVAL CLUBS

Bridgwater town has a tradition, going back to the Gunpowder Plot, for holding a carnival procession every year on the nearest Thursday to 5 November. It now draws visitors to the town in excess of 100 000 who enjoy a free show. Donations are asked for and these go to local charities. In the past, North Newton has joined in the fun with its own senior and junior clubs producing tractor-drawn floats. The senior team called themselves 'The Harvesters', whilst the juniors were known as 'Village People'. Great prestige has been attached to winning the various cups awarded in different categories. Sadly, both the clubs have ceased (the children's club in 1990), but the efforts of those involved are worthy of note – not least the parents who gave the children such enthusiastic support:

1984: 'Venice in Peril' won the John Harvey Cup.
1985: 'Children of the World' won the John Harvey Cup.
1986: 'It's Magic' swept the board with prizes, including the P.M. Druce Cup and the County Juvenile Cup.
1987: 'Flowers in the Rain' won The Ben Squibbs Cup and the P.M. Druce Cup.

The floats were built at Greenway Farm, Moon Lane and Coxhill. The Arthur Hodgert Memorial Rose Bowl is now a trophy donated to the carnival in memory of Arthur who was Club Chairman for several years.

Above: *North Newton Senior Carnival Club in the late 1940s. Left to Right, Ethel Williams, Jim Coombes, Evelyn Hutchings, Bill Whitehead, Mrs Coombes, Mrs Hawkins, Mrs Thomas, Ciss Whitehead, Ollie Adams (by post), ? (man in hat), Mrs Bartlett, ? (man in front).* Top: *'Three Wheels on my Wagon', 1979.*

115

CARNIVAL CLUBS

Below: *North Newton Senior Carnival Club in the 1970s. Left to Right: John Durman, Bob Palmer, Clarence Clatworthy, Howard Groves, Jim Clatworthy, Malcolm Carter, Steve Clatworthy, Arthur Hodgert, Edwin Hill.*

Below left: *'Children of the World' by the Junior Club 1985. Left to right, back row: Bridget Luff, Judith Roper, Jamie Collard, Penny Bowden, Gavin Holt; front: Susanne Bradford, ?, Jason Irish, Mark Hill, Andrew Hodgert, Nicky Holt, Andrew Keirle.*

Above: *'It's Magic' by the Junior Club in 1986.*

Below: *'Rainbow Fantasy' by the Junior Club in 1983.*

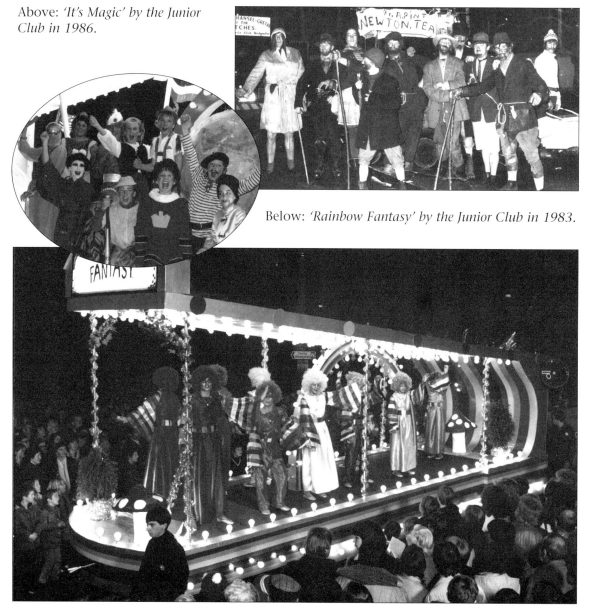

THE NEWT BEER FESTIVAL

In 1990 the Newt Beer Festival Committee held their event for the first time, little knowing what they were letting themselves in for! The original idea came from John Hesketh in response to a need to raise money for the running costs of a minibus that had been loaned to the school. So, together with other members of the PTA (Terry and Sarah Wolfe and Malcolm and Bridget Goodland), they arranged to hold the festival one Friday in July at Maunsel House. Real ale and music were on offer and sponsors were asked to contribute towards the costs. The organisers were well aware that they were taking a risk but they need not have feared – all went well and they decided to try again the following year.

Since then they have not looked back! The festival has got bigger and bigger, its reputation has widened, and it has moved location to a field on land owned by the Sellick family. The event is now run over two days with entertainment for children included on Saturday afternoons. It now involves thousands of pounds of outlay for the basic costs which include top-quality bands, stalls, drink, memorabilia, glasses and marquees. People come from far and wide, even camping overnight.

The beer is supplied mainly by RCH Breweries based at Weston-Super-Mare, which offers beers brewed from all over the country and from local brewers. The present committee includes: Frank Clegg (Chairman), Terry and Sarah Wolfe, John Hesketh, Jo Balcombe, Clare Foster, Mike and Linda Forbes-Buckingham, Rob Wood and Keith Lowe.

The school still remains the main beneficiary, but 1999 saw a change to the distribution of funds made available by the success of the festival as the committee has agreed that other local groups are also to benefit in return for providing help to keep the event running smoothly.

Mine's a pint! The Newt Beer Festival, 1999.

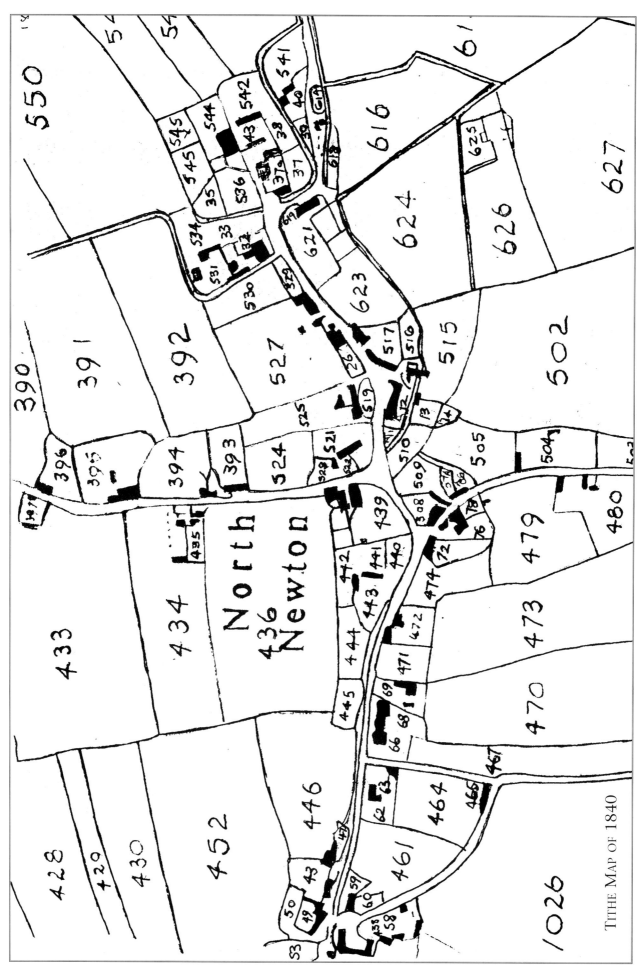

TITHE MAP OF 1840

Chapter 12: A Walk Through the Village of North Newton

The layout of the village has not changed over hundreds of years and what we see today is as shown in the Tithe Map of 1841 (almost identical to that of 1840, *shown opposite*). What has changed however, is the number of properties. Whilst many houses dating back to the 17th century still remain, most of the farm labourers' cottages of that period have, little by little, disappeared.

The Tithe Map shows large gaps of land and orchards between the properties which have now been filled with new houses, built mostly in the 20th century. The map also shows who the main landowners were in 1841. These were William Nation, the Acland family, Sir John Slade and the Vicars Choral (the Church).

In 1972, the arrival of the M5 motorway disrupted access to the village. It also meant compulsory purchase of land, resulting in the demolition of Hill View (*below*) and the loss of access to Brook Street from Spanish Hill.

Using the Tithe Map, information from various householders and Reg Price's journals to guide us, we hope to show how the village has changed over the last 160 years. Wherever possible we have explained the derivation of property names.

Hill View built in the 1930s.

PETHERTON ROAD

The village can be approached from the direction of North Petherton via Petherton Road. Before the road rises over the motorway we see **Brook Farm** which was originally thatched and probably built in the middle or late 18th century. It is now owned by the Williams family.

As we walk towards the motorway, Spanish Hill is on the left tucked away along a lane which used to be an access route to Brook Street. Two properties are located here: **Spanish Hill Farm**, where Herbie and Pat Payne live, and **Eden House**, occupied by Theresa Chant and David Askew. (Other properties on Spanish Hill are mentioned in the Brook Street section.). The name 'Spanish Hill' is thought by many to derive from an agricultural research station set up during the Spanish Peninsular Wars.

Next, after the motorway, we come to the building formerly known as **Skinners Farm** – the home of the Foster family for many years.

Historical records show that in June 1770, William Duddlestone Skynner had purchased 26 acres of land in Newton Wrothe and that he had substantial land and property at Broomfield, Cannington, Spaxton, Kingston St Mary and North Petherton. Skinners Farm came into existence, remaining in the family until sold to Jeremiah Foster early in the 19th century. It

Top: *Brook Farm.*
Above: *Bridge Farm, 1999.*

remained in the Foster family until 1979 when it was sold and the new owners then converted it for use as a commercial dog kennels and cattery. Today it is known as **Bridge Farm** and is owned by Keith and Wendy Gorman.

Willie Foster and his sisters at Skinners Farm, late 1920s.

Impens Farm.

Keeping to the left of the road we continue on to **Impens Farm**. This is a substantial building of the 16th or 17th century with ancient plasterwork and fittings, including an overmantle inscribed '1649'. It is suggested that the house may have been built (or received major repairs) after the Civil War when it was possibly the residence of a parliamentary officer. A serious fire many years ago destroyed much of the panelling and further major repairs were carried out. A post-and-truss barn near by was evidently built from oaks felled during the Civil War. The property remains in the Broughton family, with James and Jennifer in residence. James' parents, Geoffrey and Vivien Broughton, moved into the adjacent **Impens Coach House** on their retirement. **Impens Cottages** were called, at one time, Shepherds House, as they were occupied by shepherds in the employment of Albert Broughton.

The **Council Houses** were built in 1927 as a result of a proposal by ex-Police Constable John Pope and the village schoolmaster, Donald Hurd, at a meeting of the North Petherton Parish Council to build three non-parlour houses in the village. Later, after the Second World War, a further block of houses was built. Among the first to rent these properties were Mr and Mrs George Clatworthy, Mr and Mrs William Trunks, Mr and Mrs Miller, Mr and Mrs John Sellick (parents of Michael and Alan), Mr and Mrs Walter Pike, Mr and Mrs Baden-Powell, Mr and Mrs Collard, Mr and Mrs George Bond and Mr and Mrs Alfred Farthing. The houses have been renovated over the years and many have been bought by the tenants. Among the present occupants are: Michael and Margaret Duddridge, Reg, Esther and Leslie Price, and Alfred, Edward and Ella Farthing.

Opposite the council houses, on the site of an orchard, are two bungalows built by Rowland Law in 1955. **Four Winds** is owned and occupied by Rowland and Joan Law, with **Pebblestone** owned and occupied by George and Audrey Edwards.

Fackrells Farm is next in view, dating possibly from medieval times, but not later than the 16th century. Behind the house are the remains of a longhouse, now used as a garden.

The rear view of Fackrells Farm showing the site of the longhouse in the foreground.

The house at the front of the farm dates from the 1650s and is occupied by Mary and Deanna Collard-Jenkins. The adjacent new house, **Sandstones**, is owned by Mary's son, Andrew, his wife Karen, and their family. Andrew runs A.C. Services from buildings behind the farmhouse.

Opposite Fackrells Farm are three modern bungalows built on the site of three old cottages known as **Ingrams Cottages** which were owned by the late Dennis Collard-Jenkins of Fackrells Farm. Dennis sold them to David Moon who had them demolished and built the bungalows in their place. The old cottages were made of cob and could possibly have dated back to the 17th century as a Thomas Ingram is mentioned in the will of Dorothy Cheeke from West Newton dated 1618. Among the family names associated with these cottages over the years were Bond, Snook and Price. The bungalows are known as '**Juanda**', owned by David and Julia Moon, '**Mayfield**', owned by William and Barbara McLean, and '**R Place**', owned by Barry and Gloria Duddridge.

Above: *Eton Manor.*
Below: *Fackrells Farm with Sandstones behind, 1999.*

Lovings is built on the site of an old cob thatched-roof farmhouse known to have been tenanted by Clifford Whitehead (who worked for the Great Western Railway) and his wife Florence (locally renowned for making and selling her potato crisps for a penny). The farmhouse was demolished by Alan Sellick who bought it from William Foster of Skinners Farm. He built the house we see today for himself, his wife, Joyce, and their two children.

In 1989, he took down some of the old farm buildings and sold the cleared site. This was bought by the Nicholson family who then built Eton House (which has now been renamed Eton Manor) and which they later sold to Fred and Deborah Brown in 1998.

Holmlea, **Trevothan** and **Tara** were built in the 1960s on land formerly attached to Fackrells Farm. Holmlea is the home of Jeremy Rutter, Trevothan is the home of John (a retired carpenter) and Georgina (Betty) Chedzoy, and Tara is the home of Maurice, Sheila and Rachel Burgess.

Rushmead (formerly Randalls) is thought to date from the 1600s and to have once been a thatched farmhouse. In the early 20th century it was owned by Eli Pike and his family. Eli ran his market-garden business here until the late 1930s using a horse and cart to sell the produce around the area. On his death, land that he had leased reverted back to its owners and other land was sold. The property was taken over by Eli's daughter, Gertrude, and her husband. They were also responsible for a distant relative, Zena Bradford. On the deaths of Gertrude and her husband in the late 1960s, Zena remained in the house and was cared for by neighbours Doris Parsons and Levenea Radford, who lived in the cottages opposite. Zena was a zealous charity worker and when she died in 1982 in her eighties, left many legacies in her will, including £1500 each to the Village Hall and the Over Sixties Club (later the Over Fifties Club - see Village Pastimes).

Rushmead was bought by the Halliday family from North Petherton, who gave it its name and converted the outbuildings into attractive show-rooms for antiques.

In 1994 the couple moved back to North Petherton and the property was taken over by electrical contractor John Marchant, his wife, Alison, and their children. A special feature of the property is a well in the kitchen and John and Alison still have the original cider press which they rescued from the cider barn where it was being used to support the roof!

Both **Rose and Starkeys Cottages** are owned by the Broughton family, having been used to house their farm workers. They were built before 1841 using stone from the locality.

Above: *The Old Cider Press inside Rushmead.*
Below: *Rushmead.*

Starkeys Cottage is thought to have got its name from an abortive attempt at some time before 1919 by local brewers, Starkey, Knight and Ford, to turn it into a public house. The Finnimore family occupied the cottage for most of the 20th century, Gordon now being the present occupier. Rose Cottage is occupied by Ivor and Levenea Radford.

On his retirement in the late 1950s, George Lowes built **Rhodel** on land that had been attached to Rushmead. Sadly, George died in 1998, after which the property was put up for sale.

Burnt House Farm is another property that pre-dates the 1841 Tithe Map. At the turn of the century it was owned by William Bond and his family and when he moved to East Lyng in the mid 1930s it was taken over by John Sellick and his family. John was a mason by trade but turned the farm into a successful market garden. It remains in the Sellick family, but the farmhouse is at present tenanted.

The Red House was built on land from Burnt House Farm in the early 1990s for Christopher and Jean Needham.

Newton Ground was built in the mid 1980s on land purchased from John Sellick. Its name derives from the adjacent field which was used at

one time by the school and the church for sports and fêtes and also as a tennis court by the school in the 1920s. It is now owned by John Jenkins.

Belvedere and **Springfields** were built in the mid 1960s in an orchard originally belonging to Burnt House Farm. **Glenkiln** and **The Mound** are two bungalows also built in the 1960s, the former owned and occupied by Jack and Norah Chesser, and The Mound by Grace Lyne.

Puffers Cottage is said to have been named after Thomas James Adams who bought the holding in the early 20th century running it as a market-gardening business until the 1930s. He was nicknamed 'puffer' because of a respiratory problem suspected to have been brought on by mustard gas attacks in the First World War.

The cottage is thought to date from the late 17th or early 18th century. It originally had only two rooms, but at some time in the past was turned into two cottages. It was modernised in the early 1980s when the front door, which opened out on to the road, was bricked up. The present owners, Colin and Lorraine Burr, have since reinstated the doorway.

Left: *Starkeys and Rose Cottages.*

Below, inset: *Burnt House Farm on the right with the Red House and Springfield in the foreground.*

Below, main picture: *Puffers Cottage.*

Longreach, on the other side of the road, was built by Robert Pascoe in the early 1970s and probably owes its name to the fact that it is set well back from the main road up a gentle slope (or at one time perhaps a flight of steps). James and Ginny Sharratt are the present owners.

We come next to **Upfarm**. This was built in 1938 for Cuthbert Henry Godfrey and his wife Nellie who had retired from Hedging Farm. The present owners are Norman and Sybil Edwards. Sybil is a member of the WI and well known for her glass-engraving and cartography skills. The Tithe Map shows that there was previously a cottage on this site which was occupied by Benjamin Cozens but which burnt down at the beginning of the 20th century.

Opposite are two cottages, **Clyce** and **Dogwoods**, both probably built in the late 18th century. The Tithe Map shows this area as being allocated to the poor of the village, including a cottage and orchard. Clyce Cottage owes its name to former owners, the Lovell family, whose previous address was in Clyce Road, Highbridge. Joyce Lovell taught in the village school and before moving to the village, her daily journey involved taking the train from Highbridge to Durston Station then cycling from the station to school. It must have been a great relief when her parents bought the cottage in the late 1930s. The house was passed on to Miss Lovell's niece, Daphne Hewlett, and her family in 1975. Daphne, former Chairman of the Village Hall Committee, sold the house to Michael and Linda Forbes-Buckingham in 1998 when she moved with her husband, David, to Puriton. She still retains her links with the village as she continues to work in the school.

Upfarm

An interesting feature of the cottage is the elevated garden. This is at the natural level of the land and gives some idea of the effort which must have been involved in clearing the sites for various houses and the road.

Dogwoods was formerly known as 'Vicarage View'. In the early 20th century it was the home and workplace of Robert Hubbard. The house was renamed Dogwoods (the common name for the shrub, Cornus) by the present owners, the Bradbury family.

The Old Vicarage In 1987, the sale details describe the property as a perfect example of classical Victorian architecture. It was built in the early 1880s for the first vicar of the new ecclesiastical parish of St Peter, the Revd Thomas Kirby Eaton. Considering the size of the parish it is a substantial property. The financing of its

The Old Vicarage.

OLD POST OFFICE, COTTAGES AND WELL HOUSE

Above: *A 1970s aerial view of the junction at Church Road showing the school with Old Post Office Cottages on the left.*

Above: *The Well House.*
Above right: *Old Post Office Cottages.*
Right: *The Old Post Office.*

Frank Masey, his wife, Eliza, and one of their adopted sons outside Penrod (then Masey's).

construction requires further research as there appear to be two 'schools of thought' on the subject. One suggests that it was financed by a Colonel Gray who was living at Great House, Brook Street, while the other suggests that it was financed by the Revd Eaton himself.

Sarah Allen recalls a visit in the early 1990s from an Australian family called Heaton-Ellis who claimed that, in 1881, their ancestors paid for the building of the vicarage, the school and the extension to the church. Although the church had no funds to pay them back, the story goes that the family were paid for their kindness with the gift of a silver chalice. When the Heaton-Elises took in the village during a tour of Europe they asked if they might look around the house to satisfy a curiosity as to what this chalice had paid for.

The building's use as a vicarage ceased in 1974 when it was sold at auction for £7000 to Mr and Mrs Ricketts, then local teachers. Considerable renovation was carried out and the property was sold again in 1986 to a Scottish family, the Macdonald-Lockharts. It was named 'The Old Vicarage' by the present owners, Peter and Sarah Allen, who bought the property in 1988 and turned the coach house into a holiday home.

Walking further along the road we see the **Well House** opposite the school. In its time, it has been known as The Cottage, Boyers Forge and Rose Cottage. Originally a blacksmith's workshop owned by William Winter (listed in 1841), it was bought by the present owners, John and Barbara Bartlett, after extensive renovations and conversion into one house in 1992. It was renamed 'The Well House' after an old well was discovered at the rear of the house during the work.

Penrod House Many say that the house is over 200 years old, but it is not shown on the Tithe Map of 1841. However, it is shown on the Ordnance Survey map of 1887 (see North Newton in the Twentieth Century – Butchers).

Post Office Cottages appear to have been built on the site of an old bakery shown on the Tithe Map as being occupied by one Benjamin Cozens. The Ordnance Survey Map shows that the bakery had been extended and this was probably undertaken by the Maseys who owned the cottages in the early 1900s (see also North Newton in the Twentieth Century).

The end cottage was occupied until the mid 1970s, by the Yarde family. George Yarde worked as a linesman based at Durston and he walked to work every day. He was also one of the village barbers, charging children between two and fourpence, and adults four to sixpence for a cut. The property is now occupied by Linda and Lucy Defriez.

The middle cottage was the home of the Windo family for many years. Arthur Windo (son of William Herbert Windo who was the village blacksmith in the 1920s and '30s) occupied it in the 1930s and '40s. Leo and Pat Richards have made it their home since the 1970s after the renovation of the whole block by Robert Pascoe when each house was given its own entrance rather than the common path that used to run down in front of the houses. The third cottage (mentioned earlier) is now the home of Keith and Kathy Lowe.

The Old Post Office Formerly 'Porters' (see North Newton in the Twentieth Century), this building is now a house rather than a shop and is home to David, Christopher and Pippa Meikle.

CHURCH ROAD

Turning into Church Road we come upon **The Harvest Moon** public house and the **Village Hall**, next to which is a cul-de-sac of two bungalows, **Crimond**, occupied by Clarence Clatworthy, and **Little Croft**, occupied by Tony and Sylvia Rutter.

Next to the cul-de-sac is one of the oldest houses in the village, **Standards**. It is thought to have been named after the farm which used to stand near by and is likely to have been a tied farm labourer's cottage. When repairing some of the internal walls, the present owners, Richard and Josephine Horrobin, found that the original walls were made of wattle and daub, a method of construction which dates back to Saxon times when it was used for filling spaces on timber-framed houses.

Opposite Standards we see a terrace of houses. **No. 1 Church Road** is owned and occupied by Colin and Chris Perry and their family. Once a retail outlet (see North Newton in the Twentieth Century), it is now a private residence. Similarly, **Pear Tree Cottage** is previously mentioned as the old village police station and is now occupied by Sue Pottle. **Linton** is occupied by Geoff and Ann Holt and family.

We come next upon **The Old Chapel** (see Church and Chapel). It is owned and occupied by John and Sue Goulstone and their family and John runs his vintage-car-restoration business from here and has a workshop in another part of the village. The property can be seen in the old photograph (*below*) with Standards Cottage.

Church Orchard was formerly two small cottages, the last occupants being the Trunk and Whitehead families. In the 1950s the cottages were bought by Mr and Mrs Scholles who turned them into one house. Mr and Mrs Kartriber bought the property in the 1960s and it is still occupied by Joan. The building may also have been an old cider house known as 'The Blue Lamb'.

Lintomalea was built in 1988 on land that had previously been the orchard of Church Orchard. Opposite Lintomalea we find **The Willows**, on which site, before the house was built in the mid 1950s, was a row of four terraced cottages last owned by Percy Pope. The end cottage housed a shop and Reg Price was born in one of the

Above: Standards Cottage in 1999.
Below: Standards Cottage in the late 19th century (to the right of the picture). Note also the castellations on the chapel building opposite.

Above left: *No. 1 Church Road.*

Above: *The Old Chapel.*

Left: *Church Orchard.*

cottages which is now owned by Trevor and Carol Warr.

Next we see a row of four detached properties, three of which have been built since the early 1980s. **Sunnyside**, as mentioned in 'North Newton in the Twentieth Century', is the old bakery owned now by Ray and Una Barham (Una being the niece of Walter Baker).

On either side of Sunnyside we find Ray and Una's two sons and their families. James and Helen live at **Barham Court** (built in 1993), with Mark and Julia at **Julimar**. Both of these properties, together with **Sorrento**, owned by Edwin and Tina Stone, were built on land formerly belonging to Sunnyside.

On the opposite side of the road are four bungalows. Both **Shalimar** and **Gentian** were built on the site of an orchard in c.1980. **Portulaca** was built in the mid 1950s by Len and Daisy Kitts who ran a thriving nursery there until their retirement. The last bungalow, **Hedgedell**, was built in the early 1990s on land that used to be part of the nursery. It is now occupied by Andrew Goodwin.

Next to Sorrento is another of the older village properties, **Newton House**, which in all likelihood stands on the site of the courthouse for Newton Wroth, built during the reign of Elizabeth I. Prior to this there may have been another substantial building on the site. The Court of Eyre may well have stood here in the 12th and 13th centuries because a capital messuage (a large, residential property) was mentioned in 1326. In 1362 the hall and chamber were repaired with stone tiles but there is no mention made again of the house until 1450. Material may have come from the ruins of the nearby Chantry after a request was made by the church authorities to build 'an alehouse, stables and more roomy accommodation for the minor canons'. The present property is a late-16th-century building with a main hall range and a north wing. The present wing probably dates from the 18th century, but contains 17th-century windows that could have been brought from another property. The hall contains a canopied fireplace and a framed ceiling whilst the parlour has a ribbed plaster ceiling with a moulded foliage decoration.

The present owners are Andrew and Jane Smith and family. The previous owners, Gordon and Susan Stone, were given the property by Gordon's father, Edward, when he moved to North Petherton.

Court Farm was built by Gordon and Susan Stone in the mid 1980s, the farm being named after the tennis court that used to stand here.

A lane at the side of Court Farm gives access to two further properties, one new and one old. The first property, **Orchard Patch**, is an unusually-designed wood-clad bungalow built in the 1960s on part of the orchard of Church Farm. It is occupied by Joan Caygill.

Church Farm is thought to date back to the 16th century. The *Victorian History of Somerset* suggests that it may have been known as 'Pyms' in 1739 and 'Newton Place' in 1776. The house has cob walls and the east side boasts a cruck frame probably dating from the 16th century. Some refitting was carried out in the 18th and 19th centuries and the house was occupied in the late 1930s by Mrs J.B. Bickle and her husband. Mrs Bickle was a poet and authoress, who, as previously mentioned, published the book *Village of Rosemary* which features the houses and characters of the village and surrounding area. Ian and Penny Smith and family now occupy the property.

Opposite the church stand two cottages known as **The Bower** and **Elmbridge**. They are thought to have been built around 1800, probably as farm labourers' cottages. The Tithe Map shows that they were occupied by Jonathan Banfield and Eliza Franklin. They were subsequently owned by the Clatworthy family for many years. Stephen and Letitia Clatworthy were there in the early 1900s and when they moved to Coxhill Farm, their

Main picture: *Newton House.*
Centre and above: *Court Farm and Orchard Patch
(photograph taken from the church tower).*

Rear view of Church Farm.

son, Kenneth John, brought his new bride, Irene, to live in The Bower. When their family moved in the 1950s to Kings House in Maunsel Road, the property was sold to Edward Stone. It is now owned by Mark and Ann Goodwin.

In the 1920s, Elmbridge was a smallholding run by members of the Dunn family. It is now owned by Robert and Heather Morgan.

Mill Cottage stands at the bottom of Mill Hill. It may have been the rectory for the 'free chapel of Newentone'. The Tithe Map shows it as a cottage and garden occupied by William Pole. It was originally a two-bedroom cottage and for much of the 20th century it was run as a smallholding by Metford Duddridge and his family.

Colin Duddridge recalls that, during the war, Mr and Mrs Dunn and their two children stayed with them for two years because their bungalow at Chadmead had been damaged after the Army blew up some armaments. The Dunn family occupied the front room and one bedroom while the Duddridges and their three sons occupied the remaining downstairs room and bedroom. In 1989, it was sold to Frank and Julia Clegg who have substantially enlarged the property.

Mill House may have its origins in the 12th century as indicated by the first recorded reference to it, made in a grant from Richard I to William de Wrotham in 1198. Until the late 19th century, the mill was owned by various lords of the manor and major landowners, including Wrotham, Plessis, Wroth and Acland.

In the late 18th century there may well have been two mill wheels because a further water course and secondary mill pond were constructed to supplement the existing arrangement. The water course to this wheel and the remains of the wheel supports can still be seen at Mill Cottage. The Tithe Map shows that John Haines occupied the property in 1841. Today it is owned by Gordon and Anne Fraser.

The last properties in Church Road are next to Mill Cottage. Three bungalows, they were all built on the former orchard of the cottage owned by the Duddridge family. **Meleta** was built in 1967 by Metford Duddridge and is now owned by Don and Margaret Shepherd, **Capri** was built in 1968 for Colin and Jean Duddridge (who still live there), and **Caribbean** was built in the mid 1960s for Tony and Pat Duddridge (also still in residence).

The road ends at the canal but access to the four properties beyond is via the bridge and a narrow lane. This brings us to **Broadmead Farm, Whites Farm, Lower Whites Farm** and **Primrose Cottage**. Broadmead Farm was built in the late 19th century and from the early 1920s to 1983 was occupied by the Bartletts. On the death of Dennis in 1985 the property was sold to Ron and Pauline Warren who completely renovated it and installed mains electricity. In the late 1990s it was sold to Wayne and Dawn Fox. Whites and Lower Whites Farms were farmed for many years by the Fosters. George Foster took over Whites from Edwin Peach at the end of the 19th century and it remained in the family until the late 1980s when it was sold. It has had several owners since then, the present occupants being John and Ann Davies. The Fosters still own Lower Whites which is run by Colin Foster. Primrose Cottage is occupied by Brian Foster.

LOWER CHURCH ROAD

Top: *View of The Bower, Elmbridge and the side of Hedgedell from the church tower.*

Above left: *Mill House.*

Above: *Mill Cottage.*

BROOK STREET
(FORMERLY ST JOHNS STREET)

If we now retrace our steps to the centre of the village and head for Brook Street and Maunsel Road, we pass by **Smithy Cottage** (the former Post Office) on our left. This is now owned by Chris and Janet Patten.

As we turn right towards Brook Street we see **Stones Farm** in front of us. This property was built in the 17th century and the Tithe Map shows that in 1841 George Stone (from whom the farm's name derives) lived there. Since the late 1800s it has been associated with the Bartlett family, one James Bartlett being the first. He passed it on to his son, Alfred, who married Beatrice May Stone in the 1920s. The present owners are Mostyn and Heather Brown (the latter being one of Alfred's daughters).

The brook now comes into view for the first

Above: *The Pattens outside Smithy Cottage.*
Below: *Mulberry.*

time, which has been diverted from the opposite side of the road at a point where **Heather View** now stands. This diversion was necessary to avoid the flooding which still, on occasions, continues to be a problem. The brook disappears underground, flowing past Penrod across the Harvest Moon car park, down to the mill pond and on to the Levels. In the 18th and 19th centuries, before the diversion, an iron bridge was laid across the brook at Penrod. When the road was surfaced in the 1860s the changes in place today were made.

The first house on the right is **Mulberry**. Built in the mid 1800s by George Reading, it remained in the family for approximately 126 years until its sale in 1986 to the present owners, Peter and Alison Goldie. The remains of the Readings' carpenter's shop and shed were removed and Heather View was built on the cleared site. This is now occupied by Clive Singleton, but at the time of writing is up for sale.

STONES FARM

Stones Farm c.1900 (top) with Grannie Bartlett at the door and (bottom) in 1999 .

Opposite is **Brook Turn**, so named after the re-routing of the brook, commemorated by a plaque in the wall (*left*). Two cottages used to stand on the site and the Tithe Map shows that they were occupied by Thomas Stone. In the first part of the 20th century the cottages were occupied by members of the Willis and Foster families. The last family to live there was the Baker family. When they moved to No. 2 The Court, Maunsel Road, in the early 1950s, Graham Reading converted them into the house we see today and which remains occupied by Graham and his wife Althea.

We come next to a new property, **Vole House**, built in 1992 on part of the farmyard of the next property, Sellicks Farm, and now occupied by Martin and Angela Burroughs.

Sellicks Farm was also known as Brook House. It is here that Una Barham was born. The house is shown as being occupied by Robert Bell in 1841, and in the early 20th century, it was lived in by the Marks family. In the 1950s it was taken over by Reginald Edwards who ran a poultry business from the farm. The property was purchased in the early 1990s by David and Sharon Gutteridge who are in the process of renovating the building which has, of late, been somewhat neglected.

Up until the 1960s when it was demolished, there was a house known as **Homeleigh** attached to Sellicks Farm. The Tithe Map shows a path leading to Tuckerton Road at the side of the house which at this time was occupied by Jos Blackmore. It was quite a substantial building, probably dating from the 18th century or earlier and in the 1920s was divided into two properties. Among the occupants of the house have been Walter Gardner and his family (Walter was a well-known withy-worker) and Ann Whitehead.

The next property is a bungalow called **Hollies End**, so named by the previous owners, the Molloy family, who ran the North Newton Nursery which specialised in growing holly. It is now owned by Roger and Judith Grimshaw. The nursery business was sold to Simon and Denise Sharratt in 1992 and they have continued running it with access from Tuckerton Lane.

New House was built in 1990 in the yard of the adjacent **Chapel House** and is occupied by Richard and Frances Winward. Chapel House was formerly a farmhouse, and is thought to be on the site of the original chapel in the village. The Tithe Map shows that James Hurford occupied it in 1841 and for most of the 20th century it was in the possession of the Adams family, who, in addition to being farmers, were also farming contractors. The Adams family tenure ceased on the death of Jack Adams in 1977 and the property is now owned by Eric and Sandra Goddard.

Brook House was built on the other side of Chapel House's garden in 1990. It is occupied by the original owners, Kenneth and Christine Chard.

Coopers Orchard was completed in October 1982 on the site of an orchard owned by a cooper living in the adjacent property – hence the name chosen by the owners, Nick and Christine Stevens. During the construction of the house the family lived in a cottage in Maunsel Road and a mobile home on the site. The present owner is Barry Bollington.

The adjacent property, **Hillsborough Cottage**, is on the corner of Tuckerton Lane. This is where the cooper 'Tawney' Bedford lived with his sister. Tawney worked as a cooper at the Quantock Vale Cider Factory in North Petherton – the site is now occupied by Quantock House – and was also a well-known cider maker, having an apple mill and cider press in a wooden shed at the end of his garden. Kate O'Reilly and her children now occupy the cottage.

Continuing up Tuckerton Lane we come to eight starter homes, built, in 1993, as an attempt to provide low-cost housing to local people.

Further on is the new house built by the Sharratts alongside their nursery business and carrying on down the lane we come to the playing fields which were formed from the allotments and the Cricket Club.

Above: *Coopers Orchard, so named because the former orchard was owned by the village cooper.*

Right: *Brook Turn, now one property, but formerly two separate cottages.*

Below: *Sellicks Farm, birthplace of Una Barham.*

Above: *New starter homes in Tuckerton Lane.*

The Great House

Retracing our steps to the beginning of the lane at Hillsborough Cottage we encounter the imposing property of **The Great House** of which the 19th-century historian, Revd Gresswell, has the following to say:

In the Parish of North Newton there stands a house called 'the Great House', formerly the 'Court House' (it is shown as the Court House in 1809 with the tenant being Susan Dawe) [and] part of the Wrothe-Acland property till recent years and the last to be sold. In it a curious piece of old tapestry was found, which is now in the possession of Sir Thomas Dyke Acland and hanging on the Killerton staircase. The date is late 15th century, the subject religious.

Unfortunately, the National Trust at Killerton was unable to confirm this. The property has also been known as the Manor House and may be the old manor house of the Manor of Newton Wroth. Legend has it that the infamous Judge Jeffreys stayed here whilst dispensing his idea of justice after the Monmouth Rebellion. In 1950, the then tenants, the Randall family, reported that they had converted a dungeon into a darkroom. A vernacular architecture report makes the following observations:

It is a former manor house. Three upper windows and the house are C17 but may be older. Walls are 25-28 inches thick, but there are indications of an earlier house. Roof was replaced in 1800. The semi-cellar was probably a buttery. Stairs in rear projecting turret are imposing. It was rebuilt by Sir Thomas Wroth and his tenant c.1671, has been altered but retains its C17 staircase and other features. The gateway and flight of steps are c.C18. The round structure on the side of the road remains a mystery, [was it] part of a grand gate or part of a defence wall? as there appear to be arrow slits in the wall.

A map made in 1809 shows that the tenants were Susan Dawe and her family. The 1841 Tithe Map shows that the property was owned by the Acland family, with a tenant named Robert Bell. The 1891 census shows that it was then occupied by George Heal and his family. His daughter married William Whitehead who took over the farm. In the late 1940s, the Collard-Jenkins family bought it. Margaret Collard and her daughter, Susan, still occupy the house, but the adjoining land is owned and farmed by Margaret's son, John.

Steps Farm

Steps Farm owes its name to the steep flight of steps leading up to the front door. Thought to have been built around 1600, the house is of cob construction and one of the few remaining thatched cottages in the parish. In 1841, William Callow junr occupied it. Since 1919 it has been in the possession of the Foster family. Jack Foster, who died in 1991, was a well-known character in the village. He made his own cider in one of the outbuildings, using a press reputed to be over 300 years old.

Alan Bradford of Parsons Farm has fond memories of his uncle Jack and life at Steps Farm. As a young lad of seven years, Alan and his brother, Tony, needed to stay with Grannie Foster for six months as their mum was ill in hospital. In the mornings Alan milked the cows by hand, fed them, harnessed the horse and would then be told off for being late for school! He helped Jack take produce like sugar beet to Durston Station where it was transported on to Kidderminster. Jack would disappear into the Railway Inn leaving young Alan to do all the work, picking him up on the way home! Milk would be kept in churns cooled in the stream and people came to buy it by the ladle. Often, if the stream was swollen by heavy rain, the churns had to be retrieved down the road!

Jack's widow, Joyce Foster, remains in the property with her daughter, Sally.

Part of the farm has been sold to Gary and Pauline James who, at the time of writing, are building **Ivy Bank House** which is nearing completion. Meanwhile, one of the barns is being converted by Steve Poole and his wife, who have made a feature of the old cider press in the garden.

Next we come to **Gable End**, occupied by the Root family. The present owners believe the house to have been built in the 17th century. It is of cob and stone construction and, until around 1950, was thatched. A modern extension was added in the 1980s. The Tithe Map shows that there was a blacksmith's shop on the site run by William Sparks and the Roots have found the remnants of the forge in the garage. In the 1920s the house was called 'Gerean', named by the Strong family after their children Gerald and Jean. William Strong ran a carpentry business from the premises until the mid 1940s. The house was re-named Gable End by the last owner, Tim Stiles, an ex-teacher who now runs Tim Stiles Racing and lives in Durston.

Myrtle House was originally Myrtle Farm. It was built at the beginning of the 20th century by John Jenkins, who named it after a myrtle bush that was growing nearby. The first occupants were his son, Albert, and his wife, Alice, with whom John lived after he retired.

Dr David Spencer, his wife, Dorothy, and their three children lived in the house from 1985 to 1991. During that time he obtained planning permission to convert outbuildings for a new dwelling of which Christopher and Mary Lorimer are the present owners.

The Apple House is the property converted from the outbuildings of Myrtle House. The first occupants were Paul and Jeanette Western who sold it to Lynne Alcoat in 1993 and the present owners are Robert and Christina Gudge.

Churchill Farm is shown on the Tithe Map as a substantial farm, occupied by George Paine. In the 1850s it came into the hands of the Jenkinses when George Jenkins brought his family from Middlezoy to settle there. On John's retirement,

Ernest Bartlett took over the farm. The farmhouse was renovated in the early 1990s by Terry and Rita Pope (née Bartlett) and remained in their ownership until the late 1990s when Simon and Michele Cresswell bought it.

Next to Churchill Farm we see a short lane off to the right. This was originally the access route to and from Spanish Hill which was blocked after the construction of the M5 motorway. The first property on the left is **Churchill House**, formerly known as Churchill Cottage. The name was changed by the present owners so that the postman would no longer be confused as the adjacent property was also known as Churchill Cottage! It was originally a 'two up, two down' house but the present owners, Graham and Pauline Bartlett, modernised it and turned it into a three-bed-roomed house in the late 1970s, whilst retaining some of the original walls. **Churchill Cottage** is occupied by Graham's mother, Daisy.

Jaicey Farm was built in 1969 by John Collard and his wife, Pat, on a plot belonging to Myrtle House. The name derives from John's initials and he farms the land around his property and the land at The Great House where he grew up.

Churchill Farm and (top) *Churchill House.*

MOON LANE

If we continue our walk past Churchill Farm we eventually join Moon Lane where we come across two other farm properties. The first is **Greenway Farm**, built in the early years of the 20th century by Henry Durman, who used to live at Spanish Hill. The property remains in the Durman family. The farm is now occupied by Scott, his wife Fiona, and their daughter, Sophie. Fiona's parents, John and Gillian Durman, now live in **Greenway Farm Bungalow** found at the entrance to the farm from where they run a successful business having diversified into the food industry (see Farms and Farming).

Further on, over the motorway bridge, is **Parsons Farm**. David Parsons and his wife, Ellen May, built this property in the early 1900s and in the mid 1940s, the farm was taken over by Walter and Betty Franklin. On Walter's death, Alan and Pam Bradford and their daughters moved into one half of the house, whilst Alan's aunt, Betty, remained in the other. Betty still keeps herself busy producing crops for sale at the local markets and Alan farms on the land in and around the parish.

MAUNSEL ROAD

Retracing our steps back to the centre of the village by Smithy Cottage we commence our walk along Maunsel Road. Smithy Cottage straddles the corner of Petherton Road and Maunsel Road and is attached to Masey's Cottage. In 1841, three cottages stood here with a common back entrance. These were tenanted by Richard Williams, John Whitehead and Mary Squire. In the late 1960s, the middle cottage was used to enable the conversion into the two dwellings which exist today. The present owners of Masey's Cottage are Philip and Suzanne Corran.

Similarly, **Apple Tree Cottage** and **South Dene** were a block of three, although the Tithe Map shows them as two cottages occupied by Ham Day and William Muxworthy – both agricultural labourers. The present owners of Apple Tree Cottage are Peter (Nick) and Susan Dennis, whilst Antony and Amanda Baker own South Dene.

All four properties were once owned by Frank Masey from Penrod (then known as Masey's), who bought the block of three cottages in 1892 for £297. They remained in the ownership of the Maseys and their heirs until the mid 1900s.

Opposite the cottages is **Springfield House**, once a general stores run by Conrad and Emily Reading before they moved to Mulberry. The Tithe Map shows the property as a barn and barton with a cottage next to it, occupied by Sarah Fry. The present owners are Derek and Lynda Norman.

Masey's Cottage with Smithy Cottage attached.

Redstones was built by Steve Pole in 1993 on land previously part of the adjacent property. It is now occupied by Darren Eccles and Helen Stoker.

East View and Ivy Cottages were probably built in the latter half of the 19th century. East View was occupied, from the 1920s to the '60s by the West family who were wholesale vegetable traders. From 1987 to 1997 Barry and Sandy Finch owned the house and extended the property, building a swimming pool at the back. Barry and Sandy were active in village life, being members of the concert group and both serving on the Village Hall Committee. The property is now owned by Andrew Britton and Amanda Neil. Ivy Cottage is owned by Clive and Sally Caley.

On the opposite side of the road is Matravers, built in the 1970s on land which formed part of the garden of the block of cottages. Former occupants include the Ellacotts and it is now occupied by John Bainbridge and Jane Carter.

Next along is **Dunns Cottage**, known, in the mid 19th century as the Rising Sun Inn. The 1841 census shows that it was a beer house, run by Jane Bamfield and her daughter Sarah. In the late 19th century the property was taken over by Charles and Mark Dunn, who ran a masonry and building business. On the death of Eva Dunn in 1969 the property was bought by the Lawson family. They

Maunsel Rd.

converted the property into two cottages and turned the outbuildings into further living accommodation. The present owner, Peter Gilpin, has turned the old inn back into a single cottage. The Barn is now occupied by Lindsay Dade.

Wel Te Rusten (previously called Riding Light) is occupied by Phillip and Kay Taylor.

The Court These houses were built in the 1950s on the site of a much older property and are named after the Court family who built the earlier house. The Tithe Map shows that, in 1841, there was little development in this area: it shows just two cottages occupied by John Warner (he may have been a shoemaker) and John Boyer (a blacksmith). However, the Ordnance Survey Map of 1887 shows that the area had been developed into a block of houses with a courtyard at the back. This suggests that the original house was built towards the end of the 19th century. It was demolished to make way for the present properties which are now occupied by Gillian Duddridge and Howard Durbin (No.1), Stuart and Louise Boyer (No.2) and Robert and Yvonne Baker (No.3).

The next group of houses on both sides of the road was built from the 1960s onwards on open land and orchards which had, until then, remained largely unchanged since 1941. **Westlands** was built in the mid 1960s as a retirement home for Charles and Eva West from East View Cottage and the present occupants are Reginald and Kathleen Bradford. **Walton** is occupied by David Feltham, who has lived there since it was built. **Trelawne** has recently changed hands and **Welsford** was built in the 1970s, now owned by Cuthbert Coate, having been built for his mother, Edna. From the age of 11 months, Edna

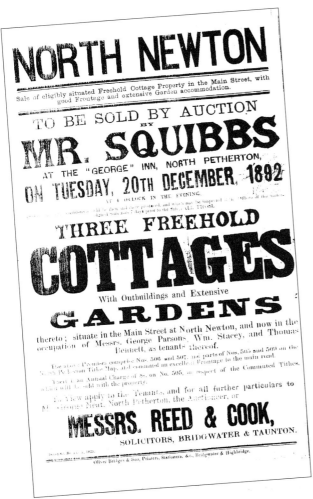

Left: Auction notice of 1892 for the three cottages which are now Apple Tree Cottage and South Dene.

SPRINGFIELD HOUSE AND REDSTONES

Top: *Springfield House.*
Above: *Redstones with East View and Ivy Cottage in the background.*

THE COURT AND HEDGEROWS

Top: *The Court.*
Above: *Hedgerows.*

Coate was brought up by the village butcher, Frank Masey, and his wife, when they lived at Penrod House. After they died, Edna inherited much of their estate. She was educated at the village school, took her part in the local community and played the church organ for many years. **Redmire** was built at the same time as Welsford and is owned by Archibald and Lindsey Abercrombie. **Hedgerows** was built at the end of the 1980s on land previously owned by a Mrs Roberts (a former owner of Redmire). The construction of the property was start-

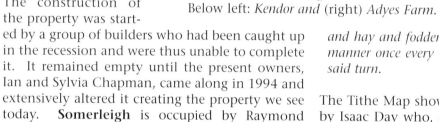

Above: *Kings House.*
Below left: *Kendor and* (right) *Adyes Farm.*

ed by a group of builders who had been caught up in the recession and were thus unable to complete it. It remained empty until the present owners, Ian and Sylvia Chapman, came along in 1994 and extensively altered it creating the property we see today. **Somerleigh** is occupied by Raymond Bollen and Jane Symner.

Opposite the above properties are two linked by family connections, **Kendor** and **Tor View**. Kendor is the home of Kenneth and Doreen Young (hence the name) and is built on the site of the old village inn, the Black Horse. In 1841, the inn was occupied by Joseph Davey and up until the late 1960s by Walter and Dorothy Ingram. Ken and Doreen purchased the property, demolished it and built their new home living in a caravan at the rear of the site whilst work was in progress. Next door, Ken and Doreen's daughter, Terena, lives with her husband, Kenneth McCallum, in Tor View. They built their home in the early 1990s on land originally belonging to Kendor.

Stone Crest was built by Hubert Stephen Clatworthy after he retired. He lives there with his wife, Susie.

We come next to another of the old properties, **Kings House** (formerly Kings Farm) which is named after a former tenant, Henry King, who sub let the property. It was probably built in the 1600s but it could be earlier and was one of the properties in the village which was used on a rotation basis by the Church for their courts. The occupants were expected to provide facilities for the court as well as hospitality, including the following:

... sufficient meat, drink and lodgings for two nights for three vicars and their steward, and hay and fodder for their horses, and so in like manner once every ten years afterwards during the said turn.

The Tithe Map shows that the farm was occupied by Isaac Day who, according to the 1841 census, lived there with his wife, three children and four servants (who were all of the Foster family). In 1875 the house and garden were leased to Mrs Hawkins. The house is described as being of cob brick and tile, containing two sitting rooms, four bedrooms, a kitchen, a cider house and wash house. It also had a gig house and stable. In 1905 the Church sold the property to William Foster, a yeoman from Durston for £1025 and in 1943 the property was sold to his sister, Eliza Letitia Clatworthy of Coxhill. In 1944, Eliza's son, Kenneth John, moved into the property with his wife Irene and family. In 1952, on the death of his mother, Kenneth and family moved to Coxhill Farm and Kings House was sold to William Denton Hawley, an artist, and Sonia Winifred Nagle (both previous tenants at Coxhill). In 1967 the property was sold to Rex and Elizabeth Chard,

who in turn sold to Tom and Helen Jeffries in 1975. We are deeply indebted to Helen for providing all the information on the house. In 1997 the property came into the ownership of David and Jackie Spackman.

Opposite Kings House is yet another of the old properties of the village, **Adyes Farm** (although its true age is not immediately apparent), which is thought to date back to Tudor times. The origin of its name remains unknown, but may come from William Frederick Adey who took the lease from William King in 1864. In 1841 William Callow senr is shown as the occupant, the census listing him as a butcher. In the early 20th century Metford Bartlett and his wife Elizabeth owned the property. By 1971 the house was occupied by Albert and Ivy Lines (whose daughter, Molly, married Michael Sellick of Burnt House Farm). Albert carried out extensive renovations on the house and it was he who discovered that it shows signs of Tudor origin. Some of the artefacts he found are now in Taunton Museum and there are remains of an old bread oven within the house. Their grandson, Bryan Sellick, and his wife, Linda, moved into the property in the early 1990s. In 1996 it was sold to Stephen and Anita Trail whose main hobby is gardening and whose gardens at Adyes are a deserved source of much envy.

It is next to Adyes that most of the latest house-building in the village has been carried out. The first of these properties, **Cricket View**, is the new home of Bryan and Linda Sellick. Next door is an identical property owned by Bryan's brother, Roger, as yet un-named. **Elland** is owned by Barrie and Alison Greenslade who moved into the property in 1995 and the remaining new properties are, at the turn of the century (*right*), at various stages of completion, including one being built by a local builder, Steve Pole, who has affectionately called the 'pile' Bed Rock!

It is worth mentioning here that the land on which the development work is taking place has been disused for many years. It was originally the site of Batts Farm, recorded to have been owned by Isaac Day. By the 1950s, it was owned by the Cousins family, and Marian Woods (née Cousins) can remember that the property had to be demolished due to irreparable structural damage. Marian now lives opposite at No.4 The Council Houses.

Next to Kings House are some bungalows and the council houses. **Freyne**, occupied by Marie Holt, and **Barnfield**, occupied by Barbara Walker, were built in the 1950s on the site of the old farmyard of Kings House. The council houses (*right*) were built in the late 1940s and are now owned and occupied by Stanley and Mavis Parsons, David and Jolene Keirle, Ernest and Rosemary Howe, Dennis and Marian Woods, Emily Foster, Robert and Julie Woods, Sandra Florés and David Henderson, and Eric and Hazel Buller.

The bungalow, **Chez Nous**, is the last occupied property in Maunsel Road. It was built in the late 1960s by the present owner, Clifford Spearing, who lives there with his wife, Catherine. Just along the road, after Chez Nous, a small lane takes you towards Coxhill. Here the first property is **Turners Farm**, occupied by Doris Collard-Jenkins. The 1841 Tithe Map shows that a barton, known as Turners, was occupied by William Winter with Thomas Whitehead living in a cottage. The farm came under the control of the Collard-Jenkins family in the early 1900s and *Kelly's Directories* show that by 1910 William Collard was running the farm and that by 1931 he had been replaced (or joined) by Albert and Reginald Collard.

Opposite the entrance to the farm used to be a thatched cottage known as **Popplehouse**, which was demolished in the early 1900s.

Coxhill Farm is a 16th-century farmhouse which in 1841 was occupied by William Whitehead. *Kelly's Directories* list the farm as being run by Francis Lang up to 1919 and in 1931 by Stephen Clatworthy – in whose family it remained until 1999 when the house was sold. Next to the farm we see a new property, constructed in 1997 for Richard (Jim) and Michelle Clatworthy. They have called the house **Liftknocker Cottage** because Michelle's father put the doorknocker on upside-down!

Over the canal bridge is **Big Bere Farm** where Terry and Sara Wolfe live and next to that is **Dunns Cottage** which is tenanted. Last but not least is **Oakmoor Farm**, the home of Trevor and Lyn Sellick and their children, Fay and Ben.

145

Batts Farm in the 1950s with Mrs Cousins at the gate, Metford Boyer on his horse and Stan Parsons on foot.

Turners Farm and (inset) *Coxhill Farm.*

Chapter 13: Local Characters

We could not write a book about the parish without taking the opportunity of recognising that it has been home to some unique people. Here we find the great and the good, and a bit of a 'rogues gallery'. There has always been a tradition of giving nicknames which have been meant as a form of affection and we have listed those which have been brought to our notice, giving an explanation (where there is one!).

'Cracker' – Francis Duddridge of Fackrells Farm.
'Puffer' – Thomas Adams of Puffers Cottage (named after him). He was a victim of a poisonous gas attack in the First World War and suffered from respiratory problems.
'Finky' – of the Bonds from Burnt House Farm.
'Bucky' – Walter Gardner of Home Leigh, Brook Street (house now demolished).
'Eagle-eye' – Charlotte Adams (née Durman), wife of Walter of Chapel Hill Farm, Brook Street. This probably does not need an explanation!
'Foozey' – Ted Foster of Steps Farm, Brook Street.

'Tish' – Alfred Bartlett of Stones Farm (father of Heather Brown). This is a corruption of 'teacher' as he was a paid monitor in his school days.
'Loach' – Henry Bartlett of Broadmead, brother of Alfred.
'Jam-Pots' – Members of the James family at Rydon.
'Rocky' – George Foster of Maseys Cottage.
'Royal' – George Foster of Whites Farm, said to be a true supporter of the royal family.
'Skinner' – Willie Foster of Skinners Farm.

Additional names of recent years include:

'Maud' – Steve Clatworthy.
'Stop-Cock' – Dave Keirle (a plumber).
'Gear-Box' – John Guerin.
'Jed' – John Durman.
'Min' – Trevor Sellick (the image of his father, Mike).
'Bodge' – Barry Finch (general builder).
'Catman' – Keith Gorman who runs the local kennels and cattery.
'JC' – John Collard of Jaiceys Farm.

Left to right: George Tilley Boyer, slaughterer (at 90 years of age), with Sid and Tom Higgins and Metford John Boyer with dog.

John Guerin at Court Farm in the 1960s.

Henry and Louisa Finnimore,
1910.

Eliza Foster, grandmother of
Willie Foster of Skinners Farm.

Mary Marks standing outside Brook House
(now known as Sellicks Farm).

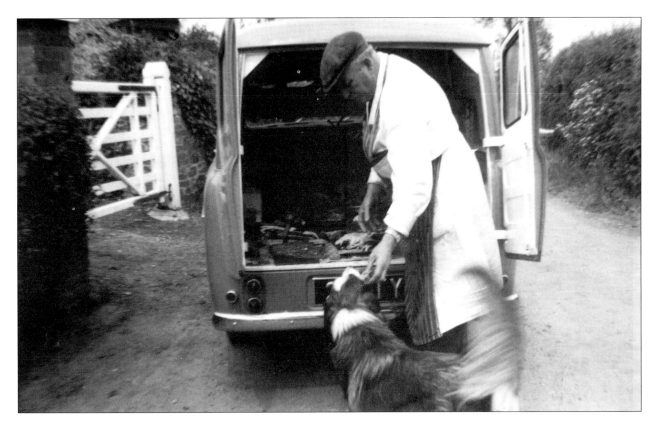

Above: *Mr Trott, local meat delivery, with Bruce the dog outside Brickyard Farm.*

Above: *'Bucky' Gardner and 'Puffer' Adams.*

Right: *Jack Foster of Steps Farm with Catcott the cow and one of eight sets of twins which she produced.*

Right: *Ian and Jenny Duddridge marry in 1972.*

Below: *Judith Brundrett Bickle, the authoress who lived at Church Farm.*

Below: *Molly Sellick as Mayor of North Petherton, 1980s. Molly is wearing the chain of office at the centre of which is displayed a replica of the Alfred Jewel.*

The Fosters of Skinners Farm, c.1904. Henry (1851-1914), Bessie (1875-1946), Willie (1900-1979) and Lily (1899-1987).

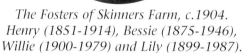

Above: *Leo and Pat Richards on their way to Stuart and Goody Scriven's wedding, 1969.*

Right: *Lady Pauline Slade at Maunsel House in 1985 with Hannibal.*

Above: *Fred and Nell Duddridge cut the cake on their 50th wedding anniversary.*

Left: *Colin and Jean Duddridge cut the cake after tying the knot in 1968.*

Right: *Andy and Karen Collard of A.C. Services, Fackrells Farm, 1980s.*

Below: *Alfred Farthing in 1995, still working at the age of 85!*

Below: *John (Jed) Durman at Greenway Farm, 1999.*

Frank Duddridge near The Mill at St Michaelchurch, 1999.

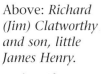

Above: *Richard (Jim) Clatworthy and son, little James Henry.*

Right: *Clarence Clatworthy with his lorry, 1999.*

Above: *Graham Reading of Brook Turn, 1999.*

Left: *Frank Clegg, Chairman of the Beer Festival Committee.*

Above: *The Habberfield 'Boys', John, Colin and Norman.*

Below: *John and Sue Goulstone with a classic car, 1999.*

Bottom: *Keith (Catman) Gorman and Wendy marry in May 1993.*

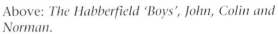

Top of this column: *The late Mike and Molly Sellick, always two very busy people.*

Above: *Jean Duddridge and Alan Bradford, 1999. There's always a funny side to everything!*

A holiday to the Isle of Man, 1981. Left to right: John (Jed) Durman, John (JC) Collard, Dave Baker, Ron Gardner, Steve (Maud) Clatworthy, Bob Pascoe.

Trevor Sellick in his tractor, cheeky as ever!

Reg Price at his typewriter.

Sandy Finch as 'Scary Spice' in the cabaret, 1997. Sue Hughes is in the background as 'Sporty Spice'.

Percy Pope inside his General Stores in Church Road.

THE FUTURE

In 1965, the North Newton branch of the Women's Institute celebrated its first anniversary by creating a scrapbook about village life in North Newton at that time. The last page is headed 'The Future?' with the comment:

At one time, quite recently, North Newton was woefully described as a dying village! This is now happily not so. In the past few years many new houses have been built, and new interests, including the formation of our WI, are rapidly developing. It is thus with hope and confidence that we look forward to a happy and prosperous future for our village.

Well, we are 35 years on and can report that the village and the surrounding parish has seen many, many more changes including the first man landing on the moon! This may not have had a direct effect on village life, but the arrival of the M5 motorway on our doorstep has certainly allowed people to travel further more quickly, the presence of commuters in the parish has increased and has,

inevitably, had an effect on the social structure of the community.

We are pleased to say that both the church and the Village Hall are still open, the Cricket Club is still thriving, the Harvest Moon is still quenching our thirsts, the skittles teams are as enthusiastic as ever and the toddlers, pre-school and the school itself go from strength to strength! Many such happy circumstances are down to a few dedicated people who can always be relied upon to muster up everyone else to support each other.

The latest projects to be tackled are linked with the millennium celebrations. A small committee of six started putting together a few ideas and passed them on to the community via a public meeting back in April 1998. Since then, some of the ideas have been dropped and new ones have emerged. A regular newsletter is produced to keep everyone up to date on progress. This book is one of the projects in which we have tried to involve as many people as possible.

Kay Robins
Penrod House, North Newton

Penrod House

ODE TO THE PEOPLE OF NORTH NEWTON

They said there's no place like it
You'll never move away,
A cheery face, a smile, a wave
Is all you need to make your day.

These characters don't realise
How funny they can be
To those who know no better
What you get, is what you see!

These genuine, lovely people
Are really 'the salt of the earth'.
At every opportunity
The air is full of mirth.

Once you've been accepted
And proved that you're OK
You're welcomed in with open arms
And maybe, you will stay.

What makes these busy people
Keep ticking as they toil
Well, as the say in Somerset,
'The answer lies in the soil!'

Everyone knows everyone,
We share our ups and downs.
It's such a close community
WHO'D WANT TO LIVE IN TOWNS!!!

Kay Robins

SUBSCRIBERS

Mr & Mrs G. Adams, Puriton

Marie Alford, Thurloxton, Somerset

Peter G. Allen, North Newton, Somerset

Sarah Anholt, North Newton, Somerset

Peter & Mary Ashton, Tuckerton, North Newton, Somerset

Pauling & Jestyn Atkins, Newport, Gwent

John & Ann Baglow, Westonzoyland, Somerset

Robert & Yvonne Baker, North Newton, Somerset

Paul & Mandy Baker, North Newton, Somerset

Ray & Una Barham, North Newton, Somerset

Mark & Julia Barham, North Newton, Somerset

J. M. & H. Barham, North Newton, Somerset

Kenneth Bartle, Melton Mowbray

Tony R. A. Bartlett, West Newton, Bridgwater, Somerset

Andrew G. Bartlett, North Newton, Somerset

Marie A. Bartlett, North Newton, Somerset

Cyril P. W. Bartlett, North Newton, Somerset

Paul Berry, Hedging, North Newton, Somerset

Penny Berry, Hedging, North Newton, Somerset

James Bond, Walton-In-Gordano, Clevedon, Somerset

Brenda Boobyer (née Farthing), North Petherton, Somerset

John & Margaret Boyer, Coxhill, North Newton, Somerset

Stuart & Louise Boyer, North Newton, Somerset

Mr N. E. Bradbury, North Newton, Somerset

Beryl, Andrew J., & Lawrence Bradbury, North Newton, Somerset

Mrs Mary K. Bradford, North Petherton, Somerset

Mr A. S. E. & Mrs P. S. Bradford, North Petherton, Somerset

Mr & Mrs Gerald Bramley, North Petherton, Somerset

Mr John Brewer, Bridgwater, Somerset

Jean Brooks, West Lyng, Taunton, Somerset

Alan, Judith, Jessica, Edward & Hannah Brown, Chadmead, North Moor, Somerset

Mr & Mrs Andrew Brown, North Petherton, Somerset

Richard, Nichola, Rebecca Brown, North Newton, Somerset

Mrs Heather Brown, North Newton, Somerset

Mrs Joan Brownlow, Bridgwater, Somerset

Valerie Broxholme, Westonzoyland, Somerset

Sandy Buchanan, Ashcott, Bridgwater, Somerset

Christopher & Sally Bult, Stringston, Holford, Somerset

Harold Bult, West Newton, Somerset

Lorraine & Colin Burr, Puffers Cottage, North Newton, Somerset

Martin & Angela Burroughs, North Newton, Somerset

Roger & Anne Carrow, Taunton, Somerset

Mrs J. M. Caygill, North Newton, Somerset

Ken & Christine Chard, Brook Street, North Newton, Somerset

Mr & Mrs J. L. Chedzoy, North Newton, Somerset

Mr J. E. & Mrs N. E. Chesser, North Newton, Somerset

Ms Trudy Chilcott, Creech-St-Michael, Somerset

Clarence Clatworthy, North Newton, Somerset

Mr & Mrs R. G. Clatworthy, North Newton, Somerset

Mr Frank Clegg, North Newton, Somerset

K. Coleman, Ffynnon Taff

Miss S. A. Collard, North Newton, Somerset

Patricia E. M. Collard, North Newton, Somerset

Deanna Collard-Jenkins, North Newton, Somerset

Diane Coram, North Newton, Somerset

Suzanne Corran, North Newton, Somerset

Simon John Cresswell, Churchill Farm, North Newton, Somerset

Annabel Darby (née Foster), formerly of North Newton, Somerset

Wendy Darch, North Newton, Somerset

Lynda & Lucy Defriez, North Newton, Somerset

Sue & Nick Dennis, Apple Cottage, North Newton, Somerset

Jeffrey Duddridge, North Newton, Somerset

Jean & Colin Duddridge, North Newton, Somerset

Roy Duddridge, North Newton, Somerset

Barry & Gloria Duddridge, North Newton, Somerset

Mr & Mrs M. Duddridge, North Newton, Somerset

Ryan David Duddridge, Bridgwater, Somerset

Mr Biddulph Dunn, North Petherton, Bridgwater, Somerset

Miss J. Durman, North Petherton, Somerset

George S. & Audrey P. Edwards, North Newton, Somerset

Mr & Mrs Sandy Evans, North Newton, Somerset

Mr Harry F. Farthing, North Petherton, Bridgwater, Somerset

Terry Farthing, Westonzoyland, Somerset

Edward J. Ferdinando, Derby

A. W. Ferdinando, Hambledon, Hants.

Robin Ferdinando, Weston-Super-Mare

Sandy & Baz Finch, Hampshire

Norman Finnimore, Newton, Somerset

The Forbes-Buckingham family, North Newton, Somerset

Reg Foster, North Petherton, Somerset

Dr Ruscombe Foster, Romsey, Hampshire

Doris Foster, North Newton, Somerset

Jo Foster, North Petherton, Somerset

Geoffrey G. Foster, North Petherton, Somerset

Mervyn Franklin, Woolavington

Gordon & Anne Fraser, North Newton, Somerset

Donald J. Gardiner, Brisbane, Australia

Patricia Gardner, Westonzoyland, Somerset

Elizabeth Acland Hood, Lady Gass, Fairfield, Stogursey, Somerset

Peter Gilpin, Dunns Cottage, North Newton, Somerset

Margery Gist (née Gardiner), Townsville, Australia

Mr David Gliddon, Wembdon, Bridgwater, Somerset

Mrs S. P. Goddard, North Newton, Somerset

Peter & Alison Goldie, North Newton, Somerset

Mrs A. Goodwin, North Newton, Somerset

Roger Goodwin, West Newton, Somerset

Andrew Goodwin, North Newton, Somerset

Keith F. & Melva D. Gorman, North Newton, Somerset

The Goulstone Family, North Newton, Somerset

Andrew & Cherry Green, Tuckerton, North Newton, Somerset

Mr & Mrs Greenslade, North Newton, Somerset

B. & K. Guerin,

J. & A. Guerin, North Newton, Somerset

Michael & Elizabeth Habberfield, North Newton, Somerset

Edward Habberfield, North Newton, Somerset

Matthew Habberfield, North Newton, Somerset

Carol & John Habberfield, North Newton, Somerset

E. Habberfield, North Newton, Somerset

Dave Habberfield, Clifton Maybank, Yeovil, Somerset

Mr R. H. Harris, North Petherton, Somerset

Colin Hawkins, Taunton, Somerset

Mr & Mrs D. Hewlett, Puriton, Bridgwater, Somerset

J. D. Hill, Cannington, Bridgwater, Somerset

Sylvia Hillman, Hedging, North Newton, Somerset

W. & A. Hodgert & H. Groves, Bridgwater, Somerset

Mrs Susan Hogg, Curry Rivel, Taunton, Somerset

Marie Holt, North Newton, Somerset

Ann & Geoff Holt, North Newton, Somerset

Christopher Hopkins, Hedging, North Newton, Somerset

Toby Horrobin, North Newton, Somerset

Ben Horrobin, Roadwater, Somerset

Nikki Horrobin, North Newton, Somerset

Margaret House, North Petherton, Somerset

R. J. Howe, North Newton, Somerset

Mrs S. Hughes, North Petherton, Somerset

Gary James, North Newton, Somerset

Mr & Mrs T. A. Jeffries, formerly of Kings House, North Newton, Somerset

Mr Richard Jenkins, North Newton, Somerset

Mr A. & Mr P. Jenkins Jenkins, North Newton, Somerset

Daisy Kitts, North Newton, Somerset

Darren M. Knight, North Petherton, Somerset

S. T. Knight, Taunton, Somerset

Terry Lavis, North Petherton, Somerset

Rowland R. & Joan M. Law, North Newton, Somerset

Paul Lawrence, formerly of 'Musgrave',Tuckerton, North Newton, Somerset

Mike Leslie, Bristol

Martyn & Nicola Lewis, Tatsfield, Kent

Katie Lewis, North Petherton, Bridgwater, Somerset

Paul S. Lock, West Hampstead, London

Andrea N. Lock, Fallowfield, Manchester

Gareth N. Lock, Bourne, Lincolnshire

Noel C. Lock, Marchington, Staffordshire

Desmond C. Lock, Fordgate, Bridgwater, Somerset

Juliet & Rebecca Lowndes, Tuckerton, North Newton, Somerset

Linda & Roger Lowndes, Tuckerton, North Newton, Somerset

The Mannion family, North Newton, Somerset

John Henry Marchant & family, North Newton, Somerset

Alistair K. Martin, North Newton, Somerset

B. Mathrick, Bridgwater, Somerset

Mr Kenneth & Mrs Terena McCallum, North Newton, Somerset

A. J. & J. N. Millett, Bridgwater, Somerset

Mrs F. C. Mockridge (née Dunn), North Petherton, Somerset

Julia Moon, North Newton, Somerset

Joyce I. Morris (born North Newton), North Petherton, Somerset

Mr & Mrs Paul J. T. Nation, Creech St Michael, Somerset

Mr & Mrs John T. Nation, Hedging, North Newton, Somerset

Mr & Mrs Martin C. R. Nation, Creech St Michael, Somerset

Mr & Mrs David J. G. Nation, Taunton, Somerset

Derek & Lyn Norman, North Newton, Somerset

North Newton C. P. School, North Newton, Somerset

Kate O'Reilly, North Newton, Somerset

Andrew & Krys Palmer, North Petherton, Somerset

Roberta Patchett, Huntworth, Somerset

Chris & Janet Patten, North Newton, Somerset

Michael Payne,

Philip Pearce, North Petherton, Somerset

Mrs Mollie Pearce (née Foster), Badgworth, Nr. Axbridge, Somerset

Ruth Peberdy, Stawell, Bridgwater, Somerset

John A. Pike, North Newton, Somerset

Mr B. R. Pitman, North Petherton, Somerset

Rachel Pope, Monkton Heathfield, Taunton, Somerset

Simon Pope, Monkton Heathfield, Taunton, Somerset

Rita Pope, Monkton Heathfield, Taunton, Somerset

Sue Pottle, North Newton, Somerset

Mrs S. W. Price, North Petherton, Somerset

Reg C. Price, North Newton, Somerset

SUBSCRIBERS

Tom & Hilary Prideaux, Chadmead, North Newton, Somerset

Alan Pryor, Banklands, North Newton, Somerset

Julie Pyne, North Atherton, Somerset

Lorraine Quick, Buckland St Mary, Somerset

Revd Rosemary Radcliffe, Thurloxton, Taunton, Somerset

Dr Nicholas Reading, North Newton, Somerset/London

Dr Catherine Reading, North Newton, Somerset/Bristol

Emily D. Retallack, North Petherton, Somerset

Mrs Carol Rhodes, Wembdon, Bridgwater, Somerset

Patricia Richards, North Newton, Somerset

Gillian W. Richards, Hedging, North Newton, Somerset

Harry Robins, St Fagans, Cardiff

Lesley A. Robins, Cardiff, Wales

Roger & Jacqui Robins, Cardiff, Wales

Alex Robins, Bristol

David Root, North Newton, Somerset

J. V. Rowland, Hedging, North Newton, Somerset

Mrs S. Rutter, North Newton, Somerset

Sylvia & Tony Rymell, Maunsel Lock Cottage, North Newton, Somerset

Patricia Saunders (née Farthing), formerly of North Newton, Somerset

M. W. Scholes, Taunton, Somerset

F. J. Scriven & Sons, North Petherton, Somerset

Mrs K Sellick, Bower Manor, Bridgwater, Somerset

Mr Nicholas Sellick, Gillingham, Dorset

Mr & Mrs Alan Sellick, North Newton, Somerset

Sir Benjamin Slade, Maunsel House, North Newton, Somerset

Nesta M. Slee (née Parsons), North Petherton, Somerset

Ian & Penelope Smith, Church Farm House, North Newton, Somerset

T. P. Smith, The Harvest Moon, North Newton, Somerset

Andrew & Jane Smith & family, Newton House, North Newton, Somerset

David & Jackie Spackman, Kings House, North Newton, Somerset

Mrs M. A. Standerwick,

Mrs Sharon L. Staunton, North Petherton, Somerset

Christine L. Stevens, North Petherton, Somerset

Gordon & Sue Stone, North Newton, Somerset

Mr Terence W. Taylor, North Petherton, Somerset

Steve Trail, North Newton, Somerset

Sarah J. Vernon, North Petherton, Somerset

Mrs Barbara Walker, North Newton, Somerset

Maureen & John Weeks, Chedzoy, Bridgwater, Somerset

David & Jane Weeks & Emily, North Petherton, Somerset

C. J. Whitehead, North Petherton, Somerset

Mr Anthony J. Whitehead, North Petherton, Somerset

Elsie Mary Whitehead, North Petherton, Somerset

Kay Wilkin, Stoke Climsland, Cornwall

Marion K. Williams, North Newton, Somerset

Patricia Williams (née Foster), formerly of North Newton, Somerset

P. J. Windo, Swindon, Wiltshire

Mr & Mrs G. Wood, Broomfield

Mr Robert Wood, North Newton, Somerset

Mr & Mrs Michael Wyatt, North Petherton, Somerset

Miss E. M. Yarde, Burnham on Sea, Somerset

Gary & Susan Young, North Newton, Somerset

Also available in the Community History Series:
The Book of Bampton Caroline Seward
Clearbrook, The Story of a Dartmoor Hamlet Pauline Hemery
The Book of Cornwood and Lutton, Photographs and Reminiscences compiled by the People of the Parish
The Ellacombe Book Sydney R. Langmead
The Book of Lamerton, A Photographic History
Lanner – A Cornish Mining Parish Sharron Schwartz and Roger Parker
The Book of Grampound with Creed Amy Bane and Mary Oliver
The Book of Manaton
The Book of Meavy
The Book of Morchard Bishop Jeff Kingaby
The Book of North Newton J.C. Robins and K.C. Robins
The Book of Plymtree, The Parish and Its People compiled and edited by Tony Eames
The Book of Porlock Dennis Corner
Postbridge –The Heart of Dartmoor Reg Bellamy
The Book of Stithians, The Changing Face of a Cornish Parish Stithians Parish History Group
The Book of Torbay, A Century of Celebration Frank Pearce
The Book of Trusham Alick Cameron
Widecombe–in–the–Moor Stephen Woods
Woodbury, The Twentieth Century Revisited compiled by Roger Stokes

Forthcoming titles in the Community History Series:
The Book of Chittlehampton
The Book of Bickington Stuart Hands
The Book of Bickleigh
The Book of Helston Derek Carter
The Lustleigh Book
The Book of Lyndhurst Roy Jackman
The Book of Meneage Derek Carter
The Book of Silverton Graham Parnell
The Book of South Tawton and South Zeal Roy and Ursula Radford

Further information:
If you would like to order a book or find out more about having your parish featured in this series, please contact The Editor, Community History Series, Halsgrove House, Lower Moor Way, Tiverton Business Park, Tiverton, Devon, EX16 6SS, tel: 01884 243242 or visit us at http://www.halsgrove.com
If you are interested in a particular photograph in this volume, it may be possible to supply you with a copy of the image.

Farm store doorways, Impens Farm.